PLAYS B
ROBERT CH

BROADWAY PLAY PUBLISHING INC
224 E 62nd St, NY, NY 10065
www.broadwayplaypub.com
info@broadwayplaypub.com

CONTENTS

About the Author v
A Note—Victor Bumbalo vi
STRAY DOG STORY 1
JERKER 47
DOG PLAYS 91

ABOUT THE AUTHOR

ROBERT CHESLEY was born 22 March 1943 in Jersey City, New Jersey and was raised in Pasadena, California. After receiving his B A in Music from Reed College in Portland, Oregon in 1965, he spent ten years teaching private school in upstate New York. During this period, he also composed prolifically. In 1976, he came out as a gay teacher and moved to New York City. During the next few years his essays and theater criticism appeared in *Gay Community News, The Advocate, Gaysweek, The San Francisco Review of Books, The Bay Guardian* and *The New York Native.*

Chesley began writing for gay theater in 1980. In that year his first play, a one-act titled HELL, I LOVE YOU was produced by Theater Rhinoceros in San Francisco. Productions of his subsequent plays followed in San Francisco, New York City and Los Angeles, as well as in cities throughout the United States and in Toronto and London. NIGHT SWEAT became the first produced full-length play to deal with the AIDS crisis, when staged by Meridian Gay Theater, New York City in 1984. JERKER OR THE HELPING HAND had its premiere at the Celebration Theater, Los Angeles in 1986. A subsequent radio broadcast by K P F K-Los Angeles of excerpts from the play prompted the Federal Communications Commission to attempt broadcast censorship for the first time since 1975. JERKER has since become Chesley's most performed play.

Chesley moved to San Francisco in the early 1980s. He resided there for most of the remainder of his life and there, on 5 December 1990 he succumbed to AIDS-related illness after a battle of almost three years. DOG PLAYS (a trilogy of one-acts) and PRIVATE THEATRICALS: MORNING, NOON AND NIGHT, written during these final years, have both been performed posthumously.

Robert Chesley leaves a literary legacy of ten full-length plays and twenty-one one-acts, as well as short stories, novels, an opera libretto, and the text for a dance-theater piece. The catalogue of his music lists more than sixty works composed between 1964 and 1976, and includes songs for solo voice, choral pieces and instrumental works. Major plays produced during his lifetime have all been published: STRAY DOG STORY by J H Press, JERKER in both the Grove Press anthology *Out Front* and in the Alamo Square Press collection *Hard Plays/Stiff Parts: The Homoerotic Plays of Robert Chesley* (with NIGHT SWEAT and DOG PLAYS).

Robert Chesley was a member of the Dramatists Guild and the Society of Gay and Lesbian Composers.

A NOTE

Robert Chesley gave voice to a generation of gay men who suddenly felt free. It was a voice of no apologies. Robert was a gentle, complicated and generous man who loved the theater. He would watch a play like a child in a trance. Ever so still with his eyes glazed and beaming. I often wonder, if Robert were in the world today, what he would make of it and what glorious words would he be adding to our culture? But I am happy to present some of his beautiful works again to his old friends and his new readers.

I'd like to thank members of the Robert Chesley Foundation and others for making this volume possible. Thank you—Michael Paller, Tom O'Connor, Sarah Schulman, Rebecca Ranson, Lorette Belglair, James Ross Smith, Nicholas Deutsch, Norman Shether, Joan Englehaupt and Kip Gould.

Victor Bumbalo

STRAY DOG STORY

An Adventure in Ten Scenes

with an introduction by
Nicholas Deutsch

to Keith

INTRODUCTION

"What a dreadful story, Granny!" I exclaimed. "Yes, it is," Granny nodded
in agreement. "And these are dreadful times, are they not?"
—Robert Chesley, *Lisa's Feet*

In the opening scene of Robert Chesley's STRAY DOG STORY, a "lonely
faggot" named Jon wishes out loud that his faithful Buddy were human
and his lover. "If people were as good-hearted as dogs," he sighs, "we
wouldn't be in the mess we're in, that's for sure." No sooner has Jon left
the room than presto! Buddy's Fairy Dog Mother appears and his and
Jon's wish is granted: Buddy is transformed into a man. And so begins
his perilous odyssey through the gay ghetto of present-day Manhattan.

Funny, angry, sentimental and disconcertingly moving, this fairy-tale play
is an original and important contribution to gay theatre. In recent years,
many playwrights have set works in the urban gay world, often with local
satirical intent. In STRAY DOG STORY, Chesley has gone further: taking for
granted the existence of that world—a community with certain shared
experience—he proceeds to explore its specific characteristics and conflicts
with the purpose of revealing something of the broader nature of the society
in which we live.

So while STRAY DOG STORY certainly doesn't avoid recognizable gay
types and stereotypes—its comic-strip mode alone would suggest their
use—it's onto something deeper than purely local satire. For one thing,
satire starts with the assumption that change, whether individual or
societal, is not only desirable but possible; for another, it maintains an
attitude of moral superiority towards the characters on the part of the
audience. But the world of STRAY DOG STORY is shown to be irrevocably
inhospitable and dangerous to the pure in heart; there is literally no earthly
way that Buddy, a canine Candide, will ever fit in or survive. And with our
loyalties divided between Buddy's uncensored needs for shelter, food and
physical warmth and the rational, uncomprehending actions of the other
characters, we must finally admit that we wouldn't—*couldn't*—behave any
differently from those who fail Buddy in the course of the play. After all,
that's the way the world is.

So the dramatic method of STRAY DOG STORY turns out to be not that
of satire, but of farce: specifically, the farce of social misunderstanding.
And farce can leave spaces for pathos and tragedy that satire cannot. What
makes the play special is that Chesley has found a way of including painful

and piteous things in the same frame as comic and charming ones. STRAY DOG STORY can move and delight an audience to an unusual degree essentially because it does not shy away from strong feeling, pleasant or unpleasant. (Indeed, rather than precluding true human feelings and values, the comic-strip form allows us to accept both horrible events and terribly human moments in a way that we might not without the safety of the comic distance.) If the ultimate social and political vision of the play is disturbingly dark and pessimistic, this arguably represents a valid reflection of the times. That Chesley manages to hold on to his humanity (and ours) seems to me a major achievement.

All of the play's theatrical and moral strengths come together in the last scene, where the writing takes on an exquisite simplicity. Here the relentless portrayal of Buddy's repeated defeats, his failure to comprehend the human world and to find in it something more than a conditional or temporary haven, finally pays off. As he and the Bag Lady—the Fairy Dog Mother in mortal guise?—huddle together in the freezing cold of Christmas Eve, the simplest acts of kindness—the sharing of food and drink, of bodily warmth and companionship—take on an aura at once magical and down-to-earth. If, as the Bag Lady says, kindness is "all we got now," for a few precious minutes that will suffice. (Of course, it is precisely because they have nothing else, can look forward to having nothing else, that the Bag Lady and Buddy can *afford* to be kind.) The past begins to slip away, old battles become memories and all that remains is the Now: the two figures hunched by the garbage cans, the crumbs of cake and the bottle of "plum wine from the summer lands." "It'll do your heart good," says the Bag Lady as Buddy drinks, and so it does. The wine also hastens his death in the winter night— but then, his heart is still a dog's heart, too pure and trusting for our ambivalent, unfeeling world. In this quiet and compassionate finale, Chesley has distilled his love for Andersen's fairy tales, and repaid the debt several times over. That bottle of wine does our hearts good as well.

Nicholas Deutsch
December, 1983

STRAY DOG STORY was first presented as a staged reading by The Glines as part of the Playwrights and Directors Series II, at the Shandol Theater in New York City, on 17 May 1982. The cast and creative contributors were:

THE FAIRY DOG MOTHER/A BAG LADY . . . . Paula Barish
JON/A MAN WHO LOOKS LIKE JON . . . . Guy Bishop
BUDDY . . . . John Finch
BRETT . . . . Frank Latson
with . . . . Don Barrington, Tod Mason, Bob Puryear, John Shelby &
Andy Torres
Narrator . . . . .Nancy Sumner

Director . . . . Nicholas Deutsch
Lighting . . . . David Pittman

STRAY DOG STORY was subsequently presented by Studio Rhino at Theater Rhinoceros, San Francisco, on 4 June 1982, the cast was:

THE FAIRY DOG MOTHER/A BAG LADY . . . . Tyler Elliott
JON/A MAN WHO LOOKS LIKE JON . . . . Rick Patton
BUDDY . . . . Michael De Martini
BRETT *(plus other roles)* . . . . .Harvey Hand
with . . . . Norbert Gabriel Breitzke & Todd Parish

Director . . . . J Kevin Hanlon

STRAY DOG STORY opened 6 January 1983, at the Shandol Theatre, presented by Meridian Gay Theater. The cast and creative contributors were:

THE FAIRY DOG MOTHER/A BAG LADY . . . . Paula Barish
JON/A MAN WHO LOOKS LIKE JON . . . . James A Harris
BUDDY . . . . John Finch
BRETT . . . . Rocco Quattro
with . . . . .Nole Cohen, Matthew Karris, Stephen Landsman & Darryl Towles

Director . . . . Nicholas Deutsch
Scenic design . . . . Campbell Baird
Costume design . . . . Mark Bridges
Lighting design . . . . Jeffrey Beecroft
Music composition & conducted by . . . . Chris De Blasio
Stage manager . . . . H Richardson Michaels

CHARACTERS & SETTING

JON, *a lonely faggot*
BUDDY, *his dog*
THE FAIRY DOG MOTHER

An S
An M
PACK OF KIDS
THIEF
BUILDING SUPERINTENDENT
FRIEND OF JON's
GAY BAR PATRONS
BOUNCER
BRETT, *an Upper East Side fag*
TWO UPPER EAST SIDE FAGS
BAG LADY *(played by the same person who plays* THE FAIRY DOG MOTHER)
MAN WHO LOOKS LIKE JON *(played by the same actor who plays* JON)
GAY DEMONSTRATORS
LEATHERMAN ACTIVIST
DEMONSTRATOR
TOM, *a gay activist*
POLICEMEN
DONDI, *a drag hooker*
TWO POLICEMEN
BRETT'S DATE
GAY RESTAURANT PATRONS

Place: Manhattan, some time in the near future

ACT ONE

Scene One

(JON's *apartment in New York City, late one summer night.* JON *is in bed, watching television.* BUDDY, *his dog, is snuggled next to him, snoozing. The news is on television: it is a brisk account of recent political atrocities, among which is the item,* "City Council member Warren Burleigh has once again refused a special police bodyguard. Burleigh, a self-confessed homosexual, has received five threats on his life since being elected to office last November." JON *sighs, and turns the television off with a remote-control box.*)

JON: Jesus! I don't think I can stand it any longer. (*He shakes his head and looks down at the sleeping* BUDDY.) What are we gonna do, boy? What are we gonna do? People are just no damned good.

(BUDDY *opens his eyes and beats his tail lovingly, looking at* JON. JON *pats him.*)

JON: Not like you, ol' sweetheart. If people were as good-hearted as dogs, we wouldn't be in the mess we're in, that's for sure. (*He snuggles his nose in* BUDDY's *fur.*) That's for sure, Buddy Boy, isn't it? *You're* the one I love, Buddy. *You're* the one that's loyal and forgiving.

(BUDDY *beats his tail happily.*)

JON: You're my best friend, Buddy. God, I wish you were a man sometimes! You'd make a wonderful lover! (*Sits up*) Shit! I could *use* a lover too!

(BUDDY *raises his head and gives* JON *a lick.* JON *giggles.*)

JON: I really love you, boy, I really do. Sorry to dump all my problems on you.

(*Another lick and a sweet whimper from* BUDDY)

JON: People are no damned good, Buddy. But *you* know that. Whoever that bastard was that left you in that dumpster out in the snow, poor pup— he must've treated you pretty bad, you're so timid. Was it bad, boy? Was it bad? Well, we've got each other now, Buddy. Yes we do. And we treat each other good. Just wish you were a man, sometimes—but not like other people. (*Sighs*) Bedtime.

(JON *gives* BUDDY *a final pat and swings himself out of bed, exits to the bathroom.* BUDDY *puts his head down. Offstage we hear* JON *piss, flush, and begin to brush his teeth. Suddenly* BUDDY *raises his head, alert, staring at a dark corner. He begins to whimper. A golden glow gradually lights the* FAIRY DOG MOTHER *standing there.)*

FAIRY DOG MOTHER: *(Like Billie Burke)* Hello, Buddy. Don't be scared. And don't bark!

*(*BUDDY *whimpers.)*

FAIRY DOG MOTHER: I'm your Fairy Dog Mother, Buddy.

(She smiles. BUDDY *beats his tail.)*

FAIRY DOG MOTHER: Once a lifetime, Buddy, every dog is granted one single wish. The wish is granted when you want it most. Most dogs wish for a nice home, but you never knew that such a thing existed, and you got it anyway. Many dogs reach a day when they wish for death, but you don't even know what that is, and, anyway, you would not wish for that now, would you? No, I sense that you have a *special* wish, something you want in the deepest corner of your heart, and that is why I am here, to grant that special wish. Tell me what your wish is.

*(*BUDDY *whimpers plaintively.)*

FAIRY DOG MOTHER: *(Moving forward to touch* BUDDY *with her wand)* Granted!

(In a flash, BUDDY *is transformed into an absolutely darling man, rather small and bouncy; he is stark naked, but is still wearing his dog collar.)*

BUDDY: *(Bouncing on the bed with great excitement)* Oh wow! Wow! Wow!

FAIRY DOG MOTHER: *(Smiling indulgently)* Be happy, Buddy! *(She disappears.)*

BUDDY: *(Scrambles off the bed and across to the bathroom on all fours)* Wow! Jon! Jon! Look what happened!

*(*JON, *startled by the racket, rushes out of the bathroom, still holding his toothbrush.)*

JON: What the fuck? Who are you?! How'd you get in here?!

BUDDY: *(Simultaneously)* Jon! Jon! It's *me*, Buddy! It's *me*! We got our wish! We got our wish! *(He rushes up to lick* JON.*)*

JON: Hey, get away from me! Get *away*!

BUDDY: *(Suddenly frightened, he scrambles over to his corner. Whimpering)* Jon! Jon! It's *me*! Really it is! Don't hurt me!

JON: *(Suddenly shocked)* Geez, you really *do* look like Buddy! Or act like him! That look you just gave me!

BUDDY: *(Hopeful)* Really it's true, Jon. It's *me*!

JON: What *is* this? Some kind of joke? Who *are* you? And where's Buddy?

BUDDY: I'm *here*, Jon! Really I am! The Fairy Dog Mother granted me our wish!

JON: Am I dreaming? Is it you, Buddy?

BUDDY: *(Bouncing up to lick* JON's *leg)* It is! It is! See, look! Here are my tags!

JON: I can't believe it!

(He ruffles BUDDY's *hair.)*

BUDDY: See, you *know* it's true!

JON: It's incredible!

BUDDY: It's wonderful!

JON: *(Leans down to look into* BUDDY's *eyes.)* It *is* you!

BUDDY: Yes! It's me!

(He gives JON *a slurpy kiss.* JON *giggles.)*

JON: Hey, can you stand up?

BUDDY: I don't know. I never tried.

JON: Try.

(He helps BUDDY *to his feet.)*

BUDDY: *(Throwing his arms around* JON*)* Oh, I *like* being a people! I can hug you!

(They hug and giggle.)

JON: *More* than just hug, Buddy!

BUDDY: Oh yes! Yes! We can make love, can't we, Jon? Wow!

JON: *(Laughing)* Yes we can! But hey! You don't need *this* any more! *(He unstraps the collar.)* You're a man, now!

BUDDY: Oh wow! Oh wow!

JON: There you go! *(He steps back from* BUDDY, *to look at him.)* We're gonna have to get you some clothes, though, tomorrow. Mine'd be too big for you.

BUDDY: Do I need clothes?

JON: Now Buddy, how many naked people have you seen on the street? Any?

BUDDY: *(Abashed)* No.

JON: So you're a person now, and you need clothes. Lucky thing I got paid today. See, no fur!

BUDDY: Oh wow! It feels funny!

JON: *(He hugs* BUDDY.*)* It feels *good.*

BUDDY: Let's snuggle in bed! Come on, Jon!

(BUDDY *leaps into bed.* JON *laughs and gets in too, realizes he is still holding the toothbrush, puts it on the bedside table, and turns the light out. The scene is lit by moonlight and city light coming in the window.*)

BUDDY: This is *nice*, Jon! I like being a man! I like snuggling!

JON: (*Cuddling* BUDDY) But, you know, there's a lot you're gonna have to learn about being a person.

BUDDY: I'll try! I'll try real hard to learn! Tell me something I have to learn!

JON: (*Pauses, stroking* BUDDY) Gee, it's hard to know where to begin! You know about clothes, now. But, gee, you're gonna need to know about money....

BUDDY: Money?

JON: It's sort of hard to explain, but you need it. We're gonna need it to get—to trade for clothing, and we're gonna need it for food. I could afford dog food for you—*just* afford it—but you can't eat that *now*.

BUDDY: Food? Meat?

JON: Yup.

BUDDY: Oh wow! Oh wow! I *love* meat! Oh wow!

JON: Yeah, well, we'll manage somehow, but—well, you're a person now, and eventually, I guess, you're gonna need a job.

BUDDY: A job? What's a job?

JON: Well, it's—like when I leave here, you know? I have to go *do* things, for money. That's called a job.

BUDDY: I don't get it.

JON: Well, I have to wait tables in a—I know, you can come along with me and see. But you'll have to behave yourself.

BUDDY: I will, I will! Wow!

JON: We don't have to worry about that now. And maybe we can get you a job in the restaurant too. We'll see.

(*Pause*)

BUDDY: (*Snuggling happily*) Jon, I love you. Really I do.

JON: I love you too, Buddy.

BUDDY: I'm so glad this happened!

JON: So'm I.

(*Pause*)

BUDDY: Jon, I'm feeling awfully good.

JON: So'm I.

(He squeezes BUDDY.*)*

BUDDY: I'm feeling so good I—I don't know, I think I'm gonna spill over!

JON: Really?

BUDDY: Oh yes! Oh wow!

JON: Hold on baby. Let's see. *(He looks under the covers.)* Hold it!

(He dives under the covers to take BUDDY's *cum.)*

BUDDY: *(Cumming)* Oh wow! WOW! AROOOOOOOOO! *(He calms down, panting.)*

*(*JON *comes out from under the covers, giggling, and gives him a big kiss.)*

BUDDY: Oh wow!

JON: You're funny.

BUDDY: Why?

JON: You sounded just like a dog.

BUDDY: I'm sorry.

JON: No! Don't be sorry! It's just funny.

BUDDY: Why?

JON: Well, not funny, exactly. It's just that I've always thought that— that cry people make when they cum is—it's from the heart.

BUDDY: I've still got a dog's heart, then?

JON: You could do worse, Buddy. You could do worse.

(He snuggles BUDDY *and they play around.)*

JON: Buddy, could you do for me what I did for you?

BUDDY: Sure! Do I just lap it?

JON: Yeah, Buddy.

*(*BUDDY *dives under the covers and laps eagerly.)*

JON: Buddy, I love you. I love you. I—

*(*JON *does not cum immediately. When he does, it is with a heart-rendingly anguished cry.)*

(Blackout)

Scene Two

(The street outside JON's *apartment—the north end of Washington Street, in the meat market district near the Mineshaft. The next morning. Two* LEATHERMEN, *an S and an M, walk down the street, crossing stage right to stage left.)*

M: I just close my eyes, it's so ugly.

S: That's shit, man! It's spectacular!

M: Sure I know it's spectacular, but that doesn't mean it's in good taste.

S: You're full of shit.

M: It's *tacky*. It looks like some fucking *bathroom*—

S: Fuck off!

M: They musta sunk a million dollars into that production, and it ends up looking like some spectacular, middle-class *nouveau-riche* bathroom, with gilded fixtures, gold-flecked tiles and gold-flecked towels—

S: Shove it.

M: Well, one thing's for sure. Nilsson's* top register is sure shot to hell. *(*Note: Prima donna's name may be changed at the discretion of the director.)*

(The LEATHERMEN *exit. A bottle is flung after them from offstage right; it crashes on the street. Two* KIDS *enter from stage right.)*

FIRST KID: *(Calling after the* LEATHERMEN*)* Fucking faggots!

SECOND KID: *(Calling back, offstage right)* Hey, come *on*, you pricks! *(To* FIRST KID*)* Shit-asses.

FIRST KID: *(Lighting a joint)* Yeah.

(He drags on the joint and passes it to the SECOND KID. *They wait. Three or four other* KIDS *enter stage right and join them.)*

SECOND KID: *(To the newcomers, passing the joint on to them)* What kept you?

THIRD KID: *(Indicating a* FOURTH KID*)* Big Whopper here had to piss.

SECOND KID: And you had to watch?

THIRD KID: *(Socking* SECOND KID*)* I ain't no fuckin' queer!

SECOND KID: No, you're the *suckin'* kind of queer!

THIRD KID: You suck your mama's pussy.

SECOND KID: Better'n suckin' faggot cock.

FIRST KID: *(Indicating* SECOND KID*)* Yeah. He run a test, see which is better.

(They laugh and move down the street, stage left.)

THIRD KID: No, I'm sorry, gentlemen. There's only one thing pussy's good for.

(They exit stage left. JON and BUDDY enter. They are both in standard Village gaymale attire, but JON's clothes are far too big on BUDDY; he looks like a clone-clown. BUDDY is bouncing around JON eagerly.)

BUDDY: Do you think people will *notice* I'm a man now?

JON: *(Stopping)* Now how're they gonna tell you weren't *always* a man?

BUDDY: Oh, I don't know. But I want people to *notice!*

JON: They'll notice you, all right, until you get some different clothes.

BUDDY: *(Abashed)* Do I look silly, Jon? Do I?

JON: *(Laughing)* Don't worry. It'll be okay.

BUDDY: Okay, if you say so.

JON: But—you've gotta calm down a bit and walk—normal.

BUDDY: But I'm so excited! I want to *play!*

JON: Yeah, but—you're not a dog any more, and you've gotta walk like a *person.* Try just walking beside me.

(They continue across the stage a bit, with BUDDY studiously trying to keep in step beside JON.)

BUDDY: *(Frowning)* Like heel?

JON: *(Stopping)* What?

BUDDY: Like I'm supposed to heel?

(JON laughs.)

BUDDY: I know you tried to teach me that once, but I couldn't get it right.

JON: Yes, I'm sorry, it *is* like you're supposed to heel. That's the way people walk.

BUDDY: Oh. I'll *try.*

(They start again, but BUDDY stops and turns to face JON.)

BUDDY: Jon, I *love* you! *Really* I do!

(He throws his arms around JON and gives him a big, slurpy kiss; JON resists a bit. At the same time, the FIRST and SECOND KID enter stage left and spot JON and BUDDY.)

SECOND KID: Hey, I think we got the genuine article here!

FIRST KID: *(Calling to JON and BUDDY)* Faggots!

SECOND KID: *(Calling back offstage left)* Hey, you prickhead! *Move* it!

(BUDDY and JON break their embrace, and BUDDY turns to look at the KIDS, and then back to JON.)

BUDDY: What are faggots, Jon?

FIRST KID: Faggot queers!

JON: *(Frozen)* Shit!

SECOND KID: Hey, you guys faggots?

BUDDY: *(Worried)* I don't like them, Jon. Let's go. *(He tugs at JON's jacket.)*

SECOND KID: Get off the street, queer boys!

JON: *(To KID)* We've as much right to the street as you—

(The other KIDS enter.)

JON: *(Seeing the other KIDS; to himself.)* Oh geez!

(The KIDS approach JON and BUDDY menacingly. The THIRD KID takes out a knife.)

KIDS: *(Variously)* Cocksuckers! Fucking queers! Faggots! You want it up the ass? Wanna suck my cock, faggot? Etc.

(JON and BUDDY turn to run. One of the KIDS nabs JON. BUDDY does not realize and runs on as the KIDS surround JON and bash him.)

BUDDY: *(As he runs)* They're gonna *hurt* us, Jon!

(He turns and does a panicked double-take to realize JON is not with him. He spins around and stops and sees the KIDS attacking JON. Rushing back into the fray)

BUDDY: You leave him alone! You leave him alone! GRRRRRR!

(He attacks with extraordinary viciousness, going right for one of the KIDS' throats and knocking him to the pavement. The THIRD KID is stabbing JON.)

THIRD KID: Die, faggot!

(JON screams and drops to the pavement; his death cry is very close to his cum cry of Scene One. One of the KIDS turns to see BUDDY mauling the throat of the KID he has knocked down.)

KID: Holy shit! He's—

(BUDDY leaps up on him and goes for his throat too; the KID tears himself away. The other KIDS have turned to see what's happening.)

KIDS: *(Variously, in sudden panic)* Holy shit! Fuckin' animal! Jesus-Mary-Mother-of-God! Let's get the fuck out of here!

(They run off, leaving one KID dead, along with JON, who is face down on the pavement, twisted.)

BUDDY: *(Looking after the* KIDS, *on all fours, protecting* JON.) Grrrr! Grrrr!
(He pants, still looking at the fleeing KIDS *and not turning to* JON.) Jon? Jon?
You okay? I guess we showed them, huh, Jon? *(He turns, still on all fours,
and smiles at* JON.) They're gone, Jon! Jon? Jon? *(Twists his head with a quizzical
look)* Jon? They didn't hurt you, did they, Jon? *(He approaches* JON *and turns
him gently over onto his back;* JON *is a bloody mess.)* Jon? Can't you speak to me,
Jon? Jon? What's the matter? *(He licks* JON's *face, then pulls away, suddenly.
He slowly gets to his feet, staring at* JON's *body.)* Oh. You're dead. They *killed*
you! Oh, Jon! *(He begins to cry.)* Oh, Jon, what am I going to *do*? *(He looks
down at* JON's *body.)* I'm gonna take you home, Jon, and I'm not ever, ever
gonna leave you, 'cause you're the man I love. *(He stoops over and takes* JON
by the shoulders, dragging him offstage.) I'll stay by you. *(Exits, dragging* JON *off)*

(Blackout)

Scene Three

*(*JON's *apartment, several days later. It is nighttime. The scene is lit only by the
bedside lamp. The window is open.* JON's *corpse, in pretty bad shape, is tucked
into bed lovingly.* BUDDY *is pacing about frantically.)*

BUDDY: What am I going to do? What am I going to *do*? Oh, Jon! I'm
starving! It *hurts*! It *hurts*! But I'll never leave you, no I won't. But Jon,
I'm so *lonesome*! I wish you could speak to me but I know you can't. Oh,
don't feel bad about that, 'cause it's not your fault you got killed. I don't
want you to worry. You've got a lot to handle right now, being dead,
I guess, and I'll be okay, so don't worry. But what am I going to *do*?
I'm starving! Oh, if I only had some *meat*! *(He stops pacing and looks at* JON.)
And oh, Jon, I *know* you can't help it, but—you don't smell so good.
It's getting worse and worse, and I don't know what to do. I opened the
window, but it doesn't seem to help. *(He approaches* JON, *fighting repulsion.)*
But that's okay, because I love you, really it is. And I want to give you all
the comfort I can. *(He crawls into bed, cuddles up to the corpse, and takes it in
his arms.)* I love you. I love you, Jon. *(He turns off the bedside lamp, and lies,
sobbing quietly.)* Oh, Jon.... *(He dozes.)*

*(The scene is lit by street light from the window. A figure appears at the window,
on the fire escape outside, and stealthily crawls into the room, heading directly for
the television. He makes a slight noise, and* BUDDY *jerks awake. The* THIEF *freezes.)*

BUDDY: Who—who are you?

THIEF: Make one move, and I'll split your belly open. *(He moves with the
television towards the window.)*

BUDDY: Why?

THIEF: I said make one move, and I'll split your belly wide open, ya get me?

BUDDY: Oh. But I need help. Can you help me? I'll help you if you help me.

THIEF: Sorry, buddy.

BUDDY: Hey! Do you know me? How'd you know it was me?

THIEF: What?

BUDDY: Oh, I need *help*! Please!

THIEF: Are you crazy?

BUDDY: Oh, I don't know. But *please* help me! See, my friend got *killed*!

THIEF: What are you talking about?

BUDDY: *(He turns on the bedside lamp. He is still holding the corpse, and looking plaintive.)* See? They *killed* him! They killed Jon!

THIEF: *(Taking in the scene)* Holy fuck! *(He puts the television down, stunned.)* Holy shit!

BUDDY: And I'm *starving*, really, but I don't want to leave Jon!

THIEF: Sorry, buddy, but I'm getting *out* of here! *(He moves towards the window.)*

BUDDY: *(Jumps out of bed and rushes to* THIEF*)* Oh *please*! I'll help you with *anything*! Just please, please get me some food so I can stay with Jon!

THIEF: You're crazy, buddy.

BUDDY: *(Sweetly bargaining)* I'll help you with the television! Jon doesn't watch it any more.... Just, can you get me some meat?

THIEF: How am I gonna do that?

BUDDY: Jon says you need *money* to get food. I can give you some money if you don't have any....

THIEF: What?

BUDDY: *(He joyfully runs back to the corpse and gets the wallet out.)* Here! Jon has money! He got paid just the day before he got killed!

(He rushes back to the THIEF *and thrusts a wad of bills at him.)*

THIEF: *(Hesitantly, taking the money)* You want meat?

BUDDY: Oh yes! Please!

THIEF: *(He pockets the money, shrugs, and takes up the television.)* Okay, buddy.

BUDDY: Oh *thank* you! *Thank* you!

THIEF: *(Going out the window)* I'll be right back.

BUDDY: Do you want help with the television?

THIEF: No, I can manage. I'm used to it.

BUDDY: Okay. Good night—and *thank* you!

THIEF: Good night. *(He goes down the fire escape.)*

BUDDY: *(Calling out the window)* See you soon, I hope. *(He turns back to* JON.*)*
See, Jon, I told you not to worry! I knew things'd work out!

(The phone rings.)

BUDDY: Oh shit! There it goes again. I wish it wouldn't *do* that!

*(He lets the phone ring and gets into bed again, snuggling up to the corpse.
The phone stops ringing.)*

BUDDY: But it'll be okay, Jon, it'll be all right.

(Suddenly there is a loud knocking on the door)

SUPERINTENDENT: *(Offstage, calling)* Hey! Anybody *in* there?

FRIEND: *(Offstage, calling)* Jon? Jon? Are you there?

(They wait. BUDDY, *frightened by the noise, slips out of bed and crouches behind it,
cowering.)*

FRIEND: *(Offstage)* Okay, I guess we gotta open it.

(The SUPERINTENDENT *unlocks and opens the door. He and a* FRIEND *of* JON's
enter. The FRIEND *flicks on the lights and takes in the scene.)*

FRIEND: Jesus!

SUPERINTENDENT: What the hell *happened* in here?

BUDDY: *(Coming out from hiding)* It's okay. Jon got killed. I mean, it's *sort* of
okay....

FRIEND: *(Shouting)* Who the fuck are you? And what did you do to Jon?

SUPERINTENDENT: He might be dangerous!

BUDDY: *(Scared, whimpering)* I—I just took Jon home after he got killed.
I tried to make him comfortable....

(The FRIEND *approaches the bed, and then backs off, repelled.)*

SUPERINTENDENT: He's *crazy!*

FRIEND: *(Shouting at* BUDDY*)* What did you *do*? What did you *do*?
Who *are* you?

BUDDY: *(He edges towards the window.)* I'm sorry.... Don't hurt me...

FRIEND: *(He rushes up to* BUDDY *and collars him. Shouting)* Hurt you?

BUDDY: Please don't!

SUPERINTENDENT: Watch it!

FRIEND: *(To* SUPERINTENDENT*)* Call the police!

(*The* SUPERINTENDENT *moves towards the phone.* BUDDY *struggles.*)

SUPERINTENDENT: (*To* FRIEND*)* Hold him!

FRIEND: I got him!

(BUDDY *bites the* FRIEND *on the hand and breaks free, runs to the window and climbs out.*)

FRIEND: (*Shocked, looking at his wounded hand*) Shit! He bit my hand!

BUDDY: (*Pausing briefly at the window*) I'll really try to come back, Jon! Wait for me! (*He exits down the fire escape.*)

SUPERINTENDENT: (*Dropping the phone*) He's getting away!

FRIEND: (*Rushing to the window*) Shit!

SUPERINTENDENT: Catch him!

FRIEND: (*Climbing out the window*) Stop! Police! Police! (*He exits down the fire escape.*)

SUPERINTENDENT: (*Climbing out after* FRIEND) Police! Police!

(*Blackout*)

Scene Four

(*The street, outside a gay disco bar, a few hours later. Music and lights come from the bar—occasionally a tambourine is heard. Guys hang around outside, drinking a beer; a* BOUNCER *guards the door.*)

FIRST FAGGOT: Did you hear?

SECOND FAGGOT: What?

FIRST FAGGOT: Another murder.

SECOND FAGGOT: Shit. Who?

FIRST FAGGOT: That guy who used to wait tables at the Three Bears. Ya know?

SECOND FAGGOT: Uh-uh. They know who did it?

FIRST FAGGOT: Looks like it was some guy he tricked with.

SECOND FAGGOT: Shit.

FIRST FAGGOT: Stabbed seven times.

SECOND FAGGOT: Shit.

FIRST FAGGOT: Found in his apartment by a friend. Been there three days.

SECOND FAGGOT: Yechh!

FIRST FAGGOT: Pretty gross. Some loony was with him.

SECOND FAGGOT: What?

THIRD FAGGOT: *(Who has been listening)* There's more to it than that.

FIRST FAGGOT: What?

THIRD FAGGOT: Seems to be a pretty sick thing.

FIRST FAGGOT: Yeah?

THIRD FAGGOT: Yeah. Seems like the guy had been gang-banged.

FIRST FAGGOT: Yeah?

THIRD FAGGOT: *After* he was dead.

SECOND FAGGOT: *Please.*

THIRD FAGGOT: *(To* FIRST FAGGOT*)* You know anything about that kind of thing going on?

FIRST FAGGOT: Nope. But it sounds hot. They tie the body up?

SECOND FAGGOT: *(Protesting)* Come *on!*

THIRD FAGGOT: That turn you on?

BOUNCER: *(Who has been listening; to* THIRD FAGGOT*)* Hey, you.

THIRD FAGGOT: Me?

BOUNCER: Yeah, you. Get outta here.

THIRD FAGGOT: I have a perfect right to be here.

BOUNCER: Move!

THIRD FAGGOT: Touch me and I'll call the police!

BOUNCER: You're eighty-sixed, sweetheart, and if you don't move your ass out of here right now, *I'll* call the police.

(The THIRD FAGGOT *exits, haughtily.)*

BOUNCER: *(To* FIRST *and* SECOND FAGGOTS*)* Shit, don't you know who that *was?*

*(*BUDDY *enters timidly, looking sad and lost.)*

FIRST & SECOND FAGGOTS: No...

BOUNCER: Well, remember next time. I'd like to tie him up and squirt lighter fluid on *his* underpants.

FIRST & SECOND FAGGOTS: *Oh.*

BUDDY: *(He approaches* FIRST *and* SECOND FAGGOTS.*)* Excuse me, I'm lost. Could you tell me where Jon's apartment is?

FIRST FAGGOT: Jon who?

BUDDY: Yeah, Jon.

FIRST FAGGOT: What's his *last* name?

BUDDY: I dunno. Does he have a last name?

FIRST & SECOND FAGGOTS: *(Looking at each other)* Right. *(They turn away.)*

BUDDY: *(Looks at the disco)* Maybe somebody knows in there.

(He tries to enter the bar. The BOUNCER *stops him.)*

BOUNCER: Where do you think you're going, buddy?

BUDDY: Can't I go in there?

BOUNCER: Let's see your I D.

BUDDY: My what?

BOUNCER: Identification, buddy.

BUDDY: Oh—I left it at home.

BOUNCER: Well, you're not going in, then. Move.

BUDDY: I didn't *mean* to...

BOUNCER: Sorry. *Move!*

BUDDY: *(Moving off; to* BOUNCER*)* But Jon told me I didn't need it any more when he took it off me! *(He goes off to one side and leans against the wall; he speaks to himself.)* I'm so tired! And I want to go back to Jon, and I want my *meat.*

*(*BRETT *comes out of the bar. He is a good-looking faggot in semi-leather drag, and he is ripped on drugs. He eyes* BUDDY.*)*

BRETT: Hey.

BUDDY: *(Looking up hopefully)* Yeah?

BRETT: Gotta light?

BUDDY: Sorry.

BRETT: Got the time?

BUDDY: No, sorry.

BRETT: Ya come here often?

BUDDY: No. I don't even know where I am.

BRETT: Ya look kinda down. Something the matter?

BUDDY: *(Smiling apologetically)* I'm lost.

BRETT: All alone in the big city?

BUDDY: Yeah, I guess that's it. I *had* a friend, but he died and I lost him.

BRETT: Sorry to hear that.

BUDDY: And I can't find my way home. You wouldn't happen to know where Jon lives, would you? Or *used* to live?

BRETT: Sorry.

BUDDY: That's okay. Thanks anyway.

(Pause)

BRETT: Say, would you like to come up to *my* place for a drink?

BUDDY: Gee, that'd be nice. I feel lonesome. You got any meat?

BRETT: Yeah, I got a nice, big piece of meat for you. Ya want it?

BUDDY: Oh yeah! Yeah!

BRETT: Hey, buddy, you really turn me on.

(He takes BUDDY *and gives him a deep tongue kiss.)*

BUDDY: *(When* BRETT *lets go)* Oh wow!

BRETT: Feeling better?

BUDDY: Oh yeah! I really like you!

BRETT: What's your name?

BUDDY: Buddy.

BRETT: I like that. I'm Brett. Shall we go?

BUDDY: Okay. Wow!

BRETT: My car's around the corner.

(They start to exit.)

BUDDY: Brett?

BRETT: Yeah?

BUDDY: Will you be my master?

BRETT: You need a master, boy?

BUDDY: Oh yes!

BRETT: *What?*

BUDDY: I said yes!

BRETT: That's "yessir!" Understand that, boy?

(They exit.)

(Blackout)

Scene Five

(The bedroom of BRETT's *Upper East Side apartment. High Tech. Spectacular view of New York City.* BRETT *enters, followed by* BUDDY, *who is obviously very pleased and eager, but is trying to behave himself.* BRETT *carefully adjusts the track lighting to just the right level, takes off his jacket, and turns around to see* BUDDY *taking off his jacket.)*

BRETT: Did I say you could do that?

BUDDY: What?

BRETT: What, *sir*!

BUDDY: *(Not understanding)* But I asked you what.

BRETT: You're supposed to say, "What, *sir*?" Don't forget the "sir."

BUDDY: Oh—sir.

BRETT: So did I say you could take your jacket off?

BUDDY: *(Shrugging good-naturedly)* Nope—sir.

BRETT: Put it back on, then, and don't take it off until I tell you to. *I* give the orders around here, understand?

BUDDY: Yeah, I guess so, sir. *(He obligingly puts his jacket back on and stands there with a question on his face.)*

BRETT: Okay. Take the jacket off.

*(*BUDDY *takes the jacket off, and smiles like a good boy.)*

BRETT: Okay, take off the rest of your clothes. You wearing a jock strap?

BUDDY: *(Looks)* Yes, sir.

BRETT: Leave it on. *(He takes off his shirt, boots and socks.* BUDDY *strips.)* You wanna drink?

BUDDY: Yes, sir.

BRETT: What d'ya drink?

BUDDY: Water, mostly, sir.

BRETT: That's all?

BUDDY: Yes, sir. Thank you, sir.

BRETT: *(Turns to go off to the kitchen)* Okay.

BUDDY: But, sir? You said you had a piece of meat for me, sir?

BRETT: Yeah. You're gonna get it, too.

BUDDY: Oh wow!—sir.

(BRETT *exits.* BUDDY *finishes stripping down to his jock strap and begins poking around, smelling things. He finds the poppers by the bedside, opens and sniffs them, looks puzzled as he recaps the bottle, and begins to reel.*)

BUDDY: Oh wow....

(BRETT *reenters with* BUDDY'*s water and a beer for himself.* BUDDY *is standing, wavering and bug-eyed.* BRETT *puts the drinks down and strides up to* BUDDY *to give him a little titwork.*)

BUDDY: *(From far away)* Ouch...sir....

BRETT: You like that, boy?

BUDDY: I don't know. It's *different*, sir....

(BRETT *gives* BUDDY *a slap on the butt, and turns to the drinks.*)

BUDDY: Ow!—sir. *(He rubs his ass, a bit baffled.)*

(BRETT *hands* BUDDY *the water and takes a swig of beer.* BUDDY *laps the water.*)

BRETT: You into piss, boy?

BUDDY: Gee, sir, I don't know, sir.

BRETT: Ever drink from a toilet, boy?

BUDDY: *(All excited)* Oh yes, sir! *(A bit sadder)* But Jon told me I wasn't supposed to, sir.

BRETT: But you like it, boy?

BUDDY: Oh yes I *do!*—sir.

BRETT: Good. *(He goes to the toy chest and busies himself with taking from it a variety of sexual toys, and arraying them on the bed. He holds up an enormous dildo.)* Ya see this?

BUDDY: Yes, sir.

BRETT: Can ya take it, boy?

BUDDY: *(Moves forward to take the dildo from* BRETT.) Gee, thank you, sir.

(BRETT *tosses the dildo on the bed;* BUDDY *makes a dive for it, and then examines it, baffled.*)

BUDDY: Is it a toy bone, sir? 'Cause I've never seen one like that if it is, sir.

BRETT: *(Thrown a bit)* Hmm?

BUDDY: Huh?—sir?

BRETT: Don't speak unless you're spoken to, boy.

BUDDY: *(Puzzled)* Okay, sir.

BRETT: *(Takes out a dog collar and leash.)* Ya like this, boy?

BUDDY: *(Suddenly very excited)* Oh yes! Oh wow!—sir. I used to have one like that, sir!

BRETT: *(He stands and puts the collar on* BUDDY, *and snaps the leash to it.)* Okay. On your knees.

(He yanks BUDDY *down to his knees.* BUDDY *shrugs happily and obliges.)*

BRETT: Okay, Buddy, ya wanted meat?

BUDDY: *(Looking up hopefully)* Oh yes, sir! I'm *starving* for meat!

BRETT: Well, get it out and suck it, boy.

BUDDY: Huh? —sir?

BRETT: *(Thrusting his crotch at* BUDDY's *face.)* I said suck it!

*(*BUDDY *figures out he's supposed to suck* BRETT's *cock, gets it out, and starts sucking.)*

BRETT: Yeah...yeah... You like that, boy?

*(*BUDDY, *still sucking, nods his head vehemently.* BRETT *clutches the back of* BUDDY's *head with one hand, face-fucking him rhythmically, and, with the other hand, pulls his belt out from the jean loops.)*

BRETT: Well, keep on suckin' boy, 'cause that feels real good. *(He lets the belt fall lightly on* BUDDY's *butt, and then raises it and lashes him.)*

BUDDY: *(Yanks back with a startled yelp, sits up on his knees and looks at* BRETT, *bewildered and hurt)* Did I do something wrong, sir? I'm sorry, sir.

BRETT: Just get back to sucking, boy. I didn't tell you to stop.

BUDDY: *(With evident misgivings, does as he is told.* BRETT *lashes him again, and this time* BUDDY *breaks free and scrambles over to a corner and accidentally pisses. Whimpering)* What'd I do? Was I naughty, sir? Don't beat me, sir. I'm sorry, I really am, sir....

BRETT: Ya don't like a little pain, boy?

BUDDY: *(In wonderment)* No, sir. I...I... *(He begins to cry.)*

BRETT: What, boy?

BUDDY: *(Sobbing)* I—I thought you were going to be a *kind* master, sir. You *did* kiss me, sir....

BRETT: *(Dropping the belt)* I don't get it. What's the matter?

BUDDY: I—I thought you were going to be *good* to me....

BRETT: Geez, am I *stoned*! I can't believe this! *(Shakes his head and looks at* BUDDY) You're really—*crying*!

BUDDY: *(Wailing)* I'm *sorry*, sir.

BRETT: *(Baffled but concerned, goes over to* BUDDY*)* That's okay—Buddy.
And you don't need to call me sir. *(He nestles* BUDDY'*s head against his legs,
comforting him and patting his head. Suddenly he raises his foot in astonishment.)*
Hey! It's wet! *You pissed on my carpet!*

BUDDY: *(Sobbing)* Oh....

BRETT: *You pissed on my new industrial carpeting!*

BUDDY: I'm sorry, sir, I didn't mean to.... I just...got scared....

BRETT: *(Hand to head)* Oh shit.

BUDDY: I *know* I'm not supposed to...and I haven't had an accident in
years...and, sir...?

BRETT: Drop the sir. What is it?

BUDDY: You—you said you had a—a big piece of meat for me, sir....
(Renewed sobbing) I mean, Brett....

(Pause)

BRETT: Oh...*food!*

BUDDY: *(Brightening)* Oh yes! You *promised* me....

BRETT: Look, get to your feet.

*(*BUDDY *scrambles up.)*

BRETT: I think all I got is some cold pizza. Will that do? I can warm it up for
you.

BUDDY: *(Jumping about enthusiastically)* Oh *thank* you! *Thank* you!

BRETT: But here. Keep still a minute. *(He takes off the collar.)* I—thought you
were—into this stuff.

BUDDY: What?

BRETT: Never mind. Look, I'm sorry about belting you. I really thought
that's what you wanted.

BUDDY: *(Puzzled)* Oh?

BRETT: Yeah, well, okay, I'm sorry. So I'll fix you the pizza, okay?

BUDDY: *Okay!*

BRETT: And then let's just—go to bed, okay?

BUDDY: Okay.

BRETT: *(Takes* BUDDY *in his arms)* This is crazy, and I don't get where you're
coming from, but I sort of like you.

BUDDY: *(Responds happily with a slurpy kiss)* I like you a *lot*, Brett. *(Hugs* BRETT*)* I want to be yours, *always*, and I'll try to be good.

BRETT: *(Pulls back a bit from the hug)* Is that your fantasy?

BUDDY: What?

BRETT: Lovers?

BUDDY: *(Happily)* Yeah, that'd be nice. *(Sensing reserve on* BRETT'*s part)* Wouldn't it?

BRETT: It's just—a pretty heavy fantasy for—a first date.

(Blackout)

END OF ACT ONE

ACT TWO

Scene One

(BRETT's *apartment, the next morning.* BUDDY *is asleep in the bed.* BRETT *enters from the bathroom, wearing a bathrobe and toweling his hair. He goes off to the kitchen and returns with two mugs of coffee. He looks a bit at* BUDDY, *who really is a pretty sight, puts the coffee on the bedside table, and then stoops down to kiss* BUDDY *awake.)*

BRETT: Good morning....

BUDDY: *(Snuggling comfortably, not awake)* Mmmm.

BRETT: *(Puts the towel down on the bed and gets into bed next to* BUDDY, *snuggling and kissing. After kissing* BUDDY) Time to get up....

BUDDY: *(Sleepily, happily)* Good morning, Brett.

BRETT: *(With another kiss)* Hi.

BUDDY: I really like you, Brett.

BRETT: Yeah? Well, I like you too. Wanna shower?

BUDDY: No thanks. But that was really *good* last night. Doncha think?

BRETT: Yeah, it was good.

BUDDY: *(Kissing* BRETT) I'm so happy. I'm so glad I'm with you. You're nice.

BRETT: Yeah?

BUDDY: Yeah. It's something I really need, you know.

BRETT: *(Giving* BUDDY *a squeeze)* Good. But now you gotta get up. *(He gets out of bed.)* Coffee?

(He hands BUDDY *a mug and takes one for himself.)*

BUDDY: Thanks. I've never tried it before.

BRETT: No? *Really?*

BUDDY: Jon used to have it. *(He sniffs the coffee, takes a sip, and then makes a wry face.)* I'm sorry, but I guess I don't like it so much. Do I have to drink it?

BRETT: No. Of course not. That's okay. *(He begins dressing; his clothes are fashionable and preppy.)*

BUDDY: *(Sits up in bed)* Are we going out for a walk?

BRETT: I gotta get to brunch.

BUDDY: Brunch?

BRETT: Yeah.

BUDDY: What's brunch?

BRETT: *(Turns to* BUDDY, *disbelieving. Pause)* It's a combination of breakfast and lunch.

BUDDY: Food?

BRETT: Yeah....

BUDDY: *(Getting out of bed)* Oh good! *(He begins hunting around for his clothes.)*

BRETT: *(Looks at* BUDDY *in silence for a while. Doubtfully)* You're not coming....

BUDDY: *(Looking at* BRETT, *puzzled)* I'm not?

BRETT: You can't!

BUDDY: I can't?

BRETT: You weren't invited.

BUDDY: Invited?

BRETT: No. (BUDDY *looks so crestfallen that he adds)* I'm *sorry*, but you see it's—well, I don't know what my friends would think of—you, dressed the way you are. I'm not even sure you could get in that way....

BUDDY: Oh.

BRETT: I'm sorry. *You* understand.

BUDDY: *(Drops his clothes and heads back to bed)* It's okay. It sounded like fun, but it's okay.

(As BRETT *stares incredulously,* BUDDY *climbs back into bed, circles three times on his hands and knees, settles down in a cozy nest of bedclothes, and smiles at* BRETT.*)*

BRETT: Buddy?

BUDDY: I'll be okay, Brett.

BRETT: What are you doing?

BUDDY: I'll wait for you here, okay? But can we go out for a walk later?

BRETT: *(Shaking his head, trying to understand)* No.

BUDDY: *(Sitting up)* No? Why not?

BRETT: You can't stay here.

BUDDY: I *can't?*

BRETT: No. Of course not.

BUDDY: I don't get it. And I can't go out for a walk with you?

BRETT: No.

BUDDY: Well, what am I supposed to do, then?

BRETT: You're—supposed to *leave.*

BUDDY: Leave? Leave you?

BRETT: Yes, of course!

BUDDY: But—I *like* you!

BRETT: Yes, but—

BUDDY: And you said you liked me!

BRETT: Well, yeah, but—you can't just move in! People don't *do* that!

BUDDY: Oh. *People.*

BRETT: Of *course* "people"! What else?

BUDDY: I see, I guess. I'm sorry. *(He gets out of bed and starts putting his clothes on.)*

BRETT: Did you drop from the moon?

BUDDY: *(Puzzled)* No...

BRETT: Well, then, what are you on?

BUDDY: On?

BRETT: What drug?

BUDDY: I don't get it.

BRETT: Never mind.

(They dress in silence for a while.)

BUDDY: *(Dressed)* Brett?

BRETT: Yes?

BUDDY: I guess this is going to sound silly, because I guess it's something I'm supposed to know, but I don't.

BRETT: What is it?

BUDDY: Where do people go?

BRETT: What do you mean?

BUDDY: I mean like me. If I'm not supposed to stay here 'cause I'm people, where am I supposed to go?

BRETT: Home. You got a home?

BUDDY: I *had* a home with Jon, and I want to go back there even though he's dead, but I got lost.

BRETT: Well, I can't help you. I wish I could, but I can't.

BUDDY: *(Brightening)* Well, maybe I'll find it if I keep looking around.

BRETT: Manhattan's an awfully big place.

BUDDY: That's okay. I got nothing better to do.

BRETT: You're funny. I can't make you out.

BUDDY: Oh? I'm trying *not* to be funny, but I guess I've got a lot to learn.

BRETT: I guess you do. Ready?

BUDDY: *(Looks around the apartment sadly, silently saying goodbye)* Yeah.

BRETT: You'll be okay?

BUDDY: I can take care of myself.

BRETT: Okay.

(They exit.)

(Blackout)

Scene Two

(The street outside BRETT's *apartment. It is the Upper East Side, and stage left there is a bus stop. A* BAG LADY—*played by the same person who played the* FAIRY DOG MOTHER, *but without the Billie Burke inflections—is standing stage right, mumbling to herself and occasionally calling out to passersby. Among the passersby are two* UPPER EAST SIDE FAGS, *very nicely dressed and groomed; they look like models, and they carry Bloomingdale's shopping bags. They enter stage right and cross to stage left.)*

FIRST UPPER EAST SIDE FAG: So I told him he had to be out of his mind.

SECOND UPPER EAST SIDE FAG: *Really.*

FIRST UPPER EAST SIDE FAG: *Me* join that messy, straggly, uncoordinated, unconvincing *mess*? I *won't!*

SECOND UPPER EAST SIDE FAG: *Really.*

FIRST UPPER EAST SIDE FAG: I mean, I don't care if Burleigh *was* gay.

SECOND UPPER EAST SIDE FAG: *Really.*

FIRST UPPER EAST SIDE FAG: That has *nothing* to do with being on the City Council. What does anyone *care* what he did in bed?

SECOND UPPER EAST SIDE FAG: *Really.*

FIRST UPPER EAST SIDE FAG: So those unkempt, unemployable gay politicos are trying to make this shooting into some kind of political cause. Claim Burleigh was shot because he was gay, that it's an attack on gay people.

SECOND UPPER EAST SIDE FAG: *Really.*

FIRST UPPER EAST SIDE FAG: So I told him where to shove *that* shit.

SECOND UPPER EAST SIDE FAG: *Really.*

FIRST UPPER EAST SIDE FAG: Candlelight march indeed! I hope it rains.

SECOND UPPER EAST SIDE FAG: *Really.*

(They exit. BRETT *and* BUDDY *enter stage right and cross to wait at the bus stop.)*

BAG LADY: *(To herself)* Murder isn't murder if you murder the right kind of people. I was murdered once. I was murdered twice, many more times. But who cares? Who the fuck cares?

BUDDY: *(Undertone)* What's she talking about?

BRETT: *(Undertone)* Nothing. Don't mind her.

BAG LADY: *(Who has overheard them preternaturally, shouting)* Nothing? Did you say nothing?

*(*BUDDY *turns, surprised.)*

BRETT: Ignore her.

(He pulls BUDDY *around so their backs are to the* BAG LADY.*)*

BAG LADY: *(To* BRETT *and* BUDDY *at first, but increasingly to herself)* Do you want to know what nothing is? Those two *rich* fags are nothing! They're nothing! Nothing, with blood on their hands! They eat the good people for dinner! For one of their goddamned fucking brunches! Bloody Marys— that's what they are! Crunch, crunch. *(She subsides into mumbling.)*

BRETT: *(Undertone)* People like that ought to be locked away.

BUDDY: Why?

BAG LADY: *(Who has heard, but to herself)* We're *all* locked away, in little cells! In little shells!

BRETT: You really don't know much about the world, do you?

BUDDY: No. I'm sorry.

BRETT: I can't figure you out. You're crazy.

BUDDY: No I'm not.

BRETT: Crazies don't know they're crazy. That's why they're crazy.

BAG LADY: *(To herself)* The leaders of this great nation! The C I A!

BUDDY: I know I must seem awfully stupid, but I'm not crazy, I just—well, I *know* this is going to sound crazy to you, but I haven't been people very long.

BRETT: What?

BUDDY: Not even a week, really.

BRETT: What are you talking about?

BUDDY: I *used* to be a dog, Jon's dog.

BRETT: *(Edgy)* You *are* crazy.

BAG LADY: If there's any truth in logic, if there's any logic in truth, the truth is it's logical to be crazy.

BUDDY: *(Shrugging)* It's the truth.

BAG LADY: It's only logic.

BRETT: Look, Buddy, I like you even though I think you're crazy—

BUDDY: Thank you.

BRETT: —and I'd like to help you out somehow, but I don't know how.

BUDDY: That's okay.

BRETT: Do you have *any* idea where this Jon lived?

BUDDY: It was near some water. I remember that.

BRETT: Was it close to where I picked you up?

BUDDY: Yeah, it was around there somewhere. I just couldn't find it.

BRETT: Well, why don't you at least come downtown with me? We're miles from there now.

BUDDY: Okay. Thanks.

BRETT: You got exact change for the bus?

BUDDY: What?

BRETT: You got any *money*?

BUDDY: I gave it all to some guy who said he'd get me some food.

BRETT: Oh.

(A MAN *who looks like* JON *enters, wearing a business suit, and stands waiting for the bus, reading a newspaper.)*

BUDDY: Jon said people trade money for food.

*(*BRETT *shakes his head and sighs.* BUDDY *shrugs and looks away, notices the* MAN.*)*

BUDDY: *(In a whisper, to* BRETT*)* Hey! That looks like Jon! I think it is!

BRETT: You said Jon was dead.

BUDDY: Yeah, but maybe he came back.

BRETT: People don't do that.

BUDDY: *(Looking at the* MAN*)* I'm almost *sure* it is! I'm gonna find out! *(He tiptoes up behind the* MAN *and stoops down to sniff his ass.)*

(The MAN *realizes someone is behind him and whirls around.)*

MAN: Hey! What do you think you're doing?

BUDDY: *(Standing up and smiling)* I thought maybe you were my friend Jon. I guess you aren't.

MAN: No, I'm not.

BRETT: I can't *believe* this!

BUDDY: *(Big grin)* But I like you anyway. *(He gives the* MAN *a big, slurpy kiss.)*

(The MAN *shoves* BUDDY *off him, but holds him by the sleeve with one hand while punching him with the other.)*

MAN: What *are* you? Some kind of fag?

BUDDY: *(Frightened and trying to pull away)* I didn't mean any harm! I just kissed you....

MAN: *(Socking* BUDDY*)* You fags think you run this city! But I've got news for *you*!

BRETT: *(Trying to restrain the* MAN*)* Hey, lay off him!

MAN: You've gone too far, you fags have, and we're gonna put you in your place! Which is *dead*, if I have anything to say about it! Police!

BRETT: Lay off! Lay off!

BAG LADY: *(Over the commotion; excited)* Inside a man is a mouse! A little, gnawing mouse, in a trap! Kill it! Kill it! It'll eat your balls away, eat them clean away! You don't need a ballbuster, buster!

MAN: You hear me? Dead! Dead! Decent people are sick and tired of you sickies! Police! Police!

BRETT: Look, you bastard, lay off him! He didn't mean any harm!

(Passersby are stopping to look, at a safe distance.)

MAN: Can't walk down the street without you fags eying me! I'll tell you what it is! It's fucking *lewd*, you sickies! Police! Police!

(A POLICEMAN *enters.* BUDDY *crumples.)*

MAN: *(Turning on* BRETT*)* Fucking *lewd*!

POLICEMAN: *(Intervening)* Break it up! Break it up!

MAN: *(He sees the* POLICEMAN *and breaks off from hitting* BRETT. BUDDY *is on his hands and knees.)* Officer, these fags made an indecent assault on me! Right here in public!

BRETT: That's not true!

POLICEMAN: *(To* BRETT*)* Shut up, fag!

MAN: I insist that you arrest them. People like that shouldn't be allowed on the streets! It's obscene!

BRETT: But it's not true.

POLICEMAN: *(To* BRETT*)* I said shut up! *(He socks* BRETT*.)*

BUDDY: Grrrr!

POLICEMAN: *(To* BRETT*)* Put out your hands, queer.

*(*BRETT *does so; the* POLICEMAN *cuffs him.)*

MAN: It's bad enough that they think they can do anything they want in public, kissing and holding hands and even—making love, but this is going too far!

POLICEMAN: *(Punches* BRETT *in the stomach;* BRETT *doubles over in pain.)* That ought to teach you!

BUDDY: Grrr! GRRRR!

(He bites the POLICEMAN *on the leg, and holds on.)*

POLICEMAN: *(Trying to shake* BUDDY *off.)* AARGHHH!!! Fucking faggot bastard!

BRETT: *(Seeing* BUDDY's *attack)* Shit.

(The POLICEMAN *reaches for his nightstick.)*

BAG LADY: *(Who has joined the onlookers)* Buddy! Buddy! Watch out!

BUDDY: *(Looks up in surprise and sees the raised nightstick; he suddenly lets go and leaps back, looks about for a split second, then breaks through the crowd and runs. The* POLICEMAN *is rubbing his leg in pain. As* BUDDY *flees)* I'm sorry, Brett! I'll try to get back! *(He exits.)*

BAG LADY: Run, Buddy! Run!

POLICEMAN: *(Starts to chase after* BUDDY, *but he is limping)* Stop! Stop or I'll shoot! Stop or I'll shoot! *(He exits.)*

BAG LADY: And he would, too, if you had a black skin! That's all I can say! Blackout! Blackout!

(Note: If BUDDY *is played by a black actor, this line should be changed to: "And he might, too! You've got a black skin!")*

(Blackout)

Scene Three

(Sheridan Square, that evening. Faggots and dykes are gradually gathering together, some bringing their own candles and others getting them from TOM, *an attractive, bearded man with close-set, fanatic eyes. Two* POLICEMEN *are on the scene. The mood is somber. A* LEATHERMAN ACTIVIST *is lecturing a* DEMONSTRATOR.)

LEATHERMAN ACTIVIST: I'll tell you where the movement people went wrong. I can tell you *exactly* where. They alienated the bar community. It's almost as if they deliberately tried to make enemies of the bar community. Their approach was pure hostility, and what did they expect? Well, they got what they were asking for, by marching through bars like Danny's, shouting, "Out of the bars and into the streets!" The bar community won't have a *thing* to do with the movement people. You don't see them at demonstrations, and that's the reason why. That's just not the way to get people to join you, by shouting at them.

DEMONSTRATOR: Uh-huh.

LEATHERMAN ACTIVIST: And I'll tell you something more. I could've told the movement people that it was going to happen. They *ought* to have known in the first place, but it's typical that they turned their anger against their own people. The irony of which is that they attacked the very people they claimed to represent. But it was like the way they alienated the lesbians. It was the same thing, really. What the *fuck* did they *expect*? *Anyone* could see it coming. It's almost like they did it deliberately. Their approach was pure hostility. The irony of which is that they got *exactly* what they were asking for!

DEMONSTRATOR: Uh-huh.

LEATHERMAN ACTIVIST: And I'll tell you something more. Read the gay press. What do you see in it? It's the same thing all over again! Look at the way the gay press writes about the bar community! They totally forget that those are the people they're supposed to be representing!

DEMONSTRATOR: Uh-huh.

LEATHERMAN ACTIVIST: The irony of which is that it's almost as if they're *deliberately* trying to make enemies of the bar community! Drive them right out of the movement! What do they expect?

DEMONSTRATOR: Yeah! Their approach is pure hostility! It's like they're deliberately trying to alienate them!

LEATHERMAN ACTIVIST: You got it! What'd I tell you?

DEMONSTRATOR: It's no wonder the bar community won't have a thing to do with the movement!

LEATHERMAN ACTIVIST: More people oughtta think like you!

DEMONSTRATOR: I mean, what the fuck do they *expect*?

LEATHERMAN ACTIVIST: Right!

(He slaps DEMONSTRATOR *on the ass; they exit together. As they pass* TOM, *he offers them candles; they ignore him.* BUDDY *enters, lost and apprehensive.)*

TOM: *(Spotting* BUDDY*)* Hi there.

BUDDY: Hi.

TOM: Join us?

BUDDY: Sure.

*(*TOM *hands him a candle.)*

BUDDY: What do I do with it?

TOM: What?

BUDDY: What are you doing?

TOM: You don't know?

BUDDY: You didn't tell me.

TOM: It's a candlelight march.

BUDDY: Oh. That sounds nice.

TOM: For Warren Burleigh.

BUDDY: That's really nice. I hope he likes it.

TOM: He's *dead*!.

BUDDY: I'm sorry. I didn't know.

TOM: He was shot!

BUDDY: That sounds awful.

TOM: Do you even know who Burleigh was?

BUDDY: No. Am I supposed to?

TOM: He was shot yesterday. He was our gay council member. He was shot because he was gay.

BUDDY: That doesn't seem right.

TOM: So this march is in memory of him.

BUDDY: Yeah?

TOM: And to protest violence against gays.

BUDDY: Gays?

TOM: Yeah.

BUDDY: What are gays? I'm sorry, I don't know.

TOM: Don't *know*?

BUDDY: No. I guess I'm supposed to....

TOM: *(Disbelieving)* Homosexuals.

BUDDY: Oh.

TOM: Do you know what homosexuals are?

BUDDY: No, I'm sorry.

TOM: *(Patiently)* Men who love other men, and women who love other women.

BUDDY: Oh. *(Brightly)* Well, I guess that makes *me* homo—what was it?

TOM: Homosexual.

BUDDY: *(Enthusiastically)* Yeah!

TOM: Gay.

BUDDY: Yeah! Gay!

TOM: So join us.

BUDDY: Yeah!

TOM: You know gays are getting killed on the streets by gangs of kids.

BUDDY: Yeah? Oh—yeah. *(Sadly)* That's what happened to my friend Jon. We were going to be lovers, but some kids killed him.

TOM: Are you kidding?

BUDDY: No, it really happened. A few days ago.

TOM: *(Putting his arm around* BUDDY*)* I'm really sorry to hear that. No wonder you seem sort of out of it. You're probably still in shock.

BUDDY: *(Beginning to cry)* And I can't find my way back!

TOM: Look, kid, stick with me. Maybe I can help you. And you really *should* march with us.

BUDDY: *(Tearfully)* Yeah?

TOM: Yeah. Think of it as being for Jon. I think he'd like that.

BUDDY: Do you?

TOM: I'm sure he would. Here, let me light your candle. It's for Jon.

(He lights BUDDY*'s candle. Many people have assembled and have lit their candles.)*

BUDDY: *(Smiling through his tears)* Thank you. I like you. You're nice.

TOM: *(Gives* BUDDY *a hug)* Gay brothers.

BUDDY: Okay.

TOM: What's your name?

BUDDY: Buddy.

TOM: Buddy. I'm Tom.

BUDDY: Hi.

TOM: Look, wait right here for me, okay? We've gotta get this march going.

BUDDY: Okay.

TOM: *(Takes a bullhorn from the box of candles, and moves to the front of the crowd. He addresses the crowd, using the bullhorn.)* Sisters and brothers! We are gathered here this evening in memory of one of our gay brothers, a great man and an indefatigable fighter for gay rights, along with the rights of other minorities and of the poor of this city. This man was shot in cold blood merely for being gay. His name was Warren Burleigh. Tonight we will march solemnly in his memory, and to protest the increasing violence against gay people which is silently condoned by our mayor and by most of the city council. We will march in memory of a great human being, who gave his life for our rights and for the rights and dignity of all peoples. But we are also honored to have among us one who will be marching in memory of someone else. Standing there among you, holding a candle, is a man whose lover was killed in the streets by a gang of punks, just this last week. Buddy, I want you to come up here and join me.

BUDDY: *(In tears and surprised, he moves up to join* TOM.*)* Gee!

TOM: *(Putting his arm around* BUDDY*)* Buddy, I want you to know that we feel deeply for you in your loss. I think it's very courageous of you to join us tonight, and I want you to know that we're all, every one of us, on your side. We love you, Buddy, we love you. And now let us all sing *We Shall Overcome. (Singing)* We shall overcome!

ALL: *(Except* BUDDY *and the* POLICEMEN, *singing)*
We shall overcome!
We shall overcome, some day!
Oh, deep in my heart,
I do believe,
We shall overcome some day!

BUDDY: *(At "I do believe," totally overcome)* Ar-ar-AROOOOOO!
AROOOOOO! AROOOOOO!

(The song falls apart.)

VARIOUS DEMONSTRATORS: Hey? What *is* this? Is this a joke? Shut him up! He's an *agent provocateur*! He's from NAMBLA! It's disgusting! Kick him out! Bastard! Asshole! Etc.

TOM: *(To* BUDDY*)* Hey! Hey! What are you doing? Shut up! Shut up! *(He shakes* BUDDY, *who continues to bay.)*

VARIOUS DEMONSTRATORS: *(Beginning to tug at* BUDDY*)* Troublemaker! Fascist pig! He's C I A! Kick him out! Shut him up!

POLICEMEN: *(They enter the fray and try to separate the* DEMONSTRATORS *from* BUDDY.*)* Break it up! Break it up!

TOM: *(Bellowing at* BUDDY*)* WILL YOU SHUT THE FUCK UP??!!

BUDDY: *(Comes to his senses and looks around, stunned)* I'm sorry.

TOM: *(Throws* BUDDY *to the ground. Contemptuously)* Crazy! *(To* POLICEMEN*)* It's okay, officers. I'll get it going again. *(Singing through the bullhorn, angrily)* We shall overcome!

DEMONSTRATORS: *(They gradually join the song, with anger in their voices, and move* en masse *to exit.)*
We shall overcome!
We shall overcome, some day!
Oh, deep in my heart,
I do believe,
We shall overcome some day!

(As the DEMONSTRATORS *pass,* BUDDY *sits huddled on the pavement, bewildered and tearful, and holding his extinguished candle.)*

A DEMONSTRATOR: *(Kicking* BUDDY *as he passes)* Dog!

(The DEMONSTRATORS *exit.* BUDDY *sits alone for a bit.)*

BUDDY: *(Looking around)* What happened? *(He gets to his feet painfully, looks offstage after the departing marchers, sighs, and limps off in the opposite direction, still holding his extinguished candle.)*

(Blackout)

Scene Four

(West Street, later that night. DONDI, *a black drag hooker, is out strutting her stuff for the passing cars. The two* LEATHERMEN *from* ACT ONE, *Scene Two, enter and cross; the M is hooded and in chaps, bare-assed, and is being led by a chain held by the S.)*

S: *(As they pass* DONDI*)* 'Lo, Dondi.

DONDI: Evenin', boys. Out for a good time?

S: Only the best.

DONDI: *Second* best, honey. You want the best, you come to *royalty*.

(The S nods and the pair exits. BUDDY *enters, limping, still holding his candle.)*

DONDI: *(To* BUDDY*)* Evenin'.

BUDDY: *(Surprised)* Hi.

DONDI: You okay, child?

BUDDY: Yeah, I guess I'm okay.

DONDI: Looks to me like you got hurt.

BUDDY: Yeah, I guess I did.

DONDI: What happened?

BUDDY: My foot's swelling up. It hurts.

DONDI: How'd you hurt it?

BUDDY: Some people kicked me.

DONDI: *Who* did that to you?

BUDDY: Some people who said they loved me.

DONDI: *(Laughing)* Ain't *that* the way it is!

BUDDY: Is it?

DONDI: *Always*, honey, *always*.

BUDDY: *Jon* didn't kick me.

DONDI: Jon was exceptional.

BUDDY: *(Hopeful, slightly excited)* You know Jon?

DONDI: Let me tell you, I've known *lots* of johns. And if your john didn't kick you, he was the *exception*.

BUDDY: *(Sadly)* Well, he didn't. He was good to me.

DONDI: I tell you, the last john I had, you know what he did to me?

BUDDY: No.

DONDI: Wouldn't pay, pulled a knife on me, tried to rob me. So I jumped from the car and told him his cock wasn't significant enough for me to pick my nose with.

BUDDY: Gee.

DONDI: I shouldda cut it off and thrown it in his face. Say, my name's Dondi.

BUDDY: Hi. I'm Buddy.

DONDI: Whatcha doin', Buddy, prowlin' around the streets like a lonesome dog?

BUDDY: I guess that's it. I can't find my way back to Jon.

DONDI: What's the candle for?

BUDDY: This?

DONDI: Yeah.

BUDDY: Somebody told me it was for Jon, that Jon wanted me to carry it. But it hasn't helped me any yet. And I don't understand. *(Breaking down)* There's so much I don't understand!

DONDI: Now, child, don't let it distress you.

BUDDY: I haven't been people very long, and I get so confused 'cause I don't know what I'm supposed to do and it seems I'm always doing the wrong thing 'cause I don't know any better. I wish I was a dog again, 'cause none of this would've happened and I'd still have Jon, and I miss him, and he loved me and fed me, and that's all I ever wanted—

DONDI: That's okay, child.

BUDDY: — 'cept I wanted to be a man 'cause Jon wanted that, he said he wanted a man to love.

DONDI: Here, child, let's light your candle, okay? Maybe it'll help.

BUDDY: Yeah?

DONDI: Sure. Worth a try.

(She lights BUDDY's *candle.)*

BUDDY: Thanks.

DONDI: Think nothing of it.

BUDDY: You're nice. And you're awfully pretty.

DONDI: Why, thank you, child. I do what I can. Say, you hungry? You look like you could use a meal or two.

BUDDY: Yeah, I'm awfully hungry.

DONDI: Well, why don't ya come along with me, and I'll treat you to a feast at the New Silver Dollar, okay? I got my earnings.

BUDDY: Gee, thanks, really. That's awfully kind of you.

DONDI: Think nothing of it. It's this way.

(They begin to cross to stage left.)

BUDDY: What they got to eat there? Meat?

DONDI: *(Red lights flash from offstage left. She sees the lights and freezes.)* Shit!

BUDDY: *(Thinking this is the answer to his question, mildly surprised)* Oh.

(Two POLICEMEN run onstage to grab DONDI; she makes a brief run for it, but is nabbed. BUDDY stands to one side, bewildered.)

FIRST POLICEMAN: *(Handcuffing DONDI)* Okay, pervert! It's off to Rikers!

DONDI: I haven't done a thing.

SECOND POLICEMAN: *(Ripping DONDI's wig off)* Solicitation and possession!

DONDI: Get your greasy hands off me, pig! You can't prove a thing!

FIRST POLICEMAN: We don't have to, pervert!

DONDI: *(Shouting)* And you call me a pervert?! You wanna know what pervert is? *You're* the perverts around here! I know I ain't gonna get no *justice* from the likes of perverts like *you*! It's *pervert* justice I'm gonna get! 'Cause white boys like you perverted all the justice there ever was in this country!

FIRST POLICEMAN: *(Socking DONDI in the belly)* Shut up, sickie!

(DONDI doubles over in pain. The SECOND POLICEMAN brains her with his nightstick, and she falls to the ground.)

BUDDY: Hey! That's my friend—

SECOND POLICEMAN: Shut up, buddy, or we'll haul you in too.

(They drag DONDI's inert body offstage left. We hear car doors slam and the car pull away.)

BUDDY: *(Stands stunned)* I don't get it. What's justice?

(Blackout)

Scene Five

(The street, several months later. Nighttime. It is Christmas Eve, and it is bitterly cold. Stage right is the Three Bears, the gay restaurant where JON used to work; through the frosted, decorated windows we can see the happy, warm, drunk PATRONS inside, including BRETT. Stage left are several overflowing garbage cans, and huddled next to these, freezing to death, is the BAG LADY of ACT TWO, Scene Two.)

BAG LADY: *(To herself)* 'Tis the season when we like to remember the neediest. 'Tis the season to be jolly. 'Tis the season of giving. 'Tis the season of love. Little white children are all in their beds, visions of sugarplums fill their blond heads, and in the morning they'll creep downstairs wearing their warm Doctor Dentons, and find Mommy broken into two pieces underneath the Christmas tree, with her head on wrong and her glassy dead eyes staring up at the pretty twinkling lights. And Daddy's in the downstairs bathroom shitting his guts out and puking blood. But by breakfast all will be well again, all will be well and warm and happy. Or so it seems, so it seems. Oh-oh. Here comes trouble.

(The KIDS *from* ACT ONE, *Scene Two, enter, drunk and huddling themselves against the cold.)*

KIDS: *(Singing)* We wish you a Merry Christmas!
We wish you a Merry Christmas!
We wish you a Merry Christmas,
And a Happy New Year!

(As they pass, the KIDS *kick the* BAG LADY's *bags all over the place, and add a few kicks to her as well.)*

BAG LADY: *(Protesting as the* KIDS *attack her)* You're *nothing!* You're *nothing!* Do you know that? You're nothing, with boots that *kick!*

(The KIDS *exit, still singing.)*

BAG LADY: *(Calling after the* KIDS*)* Does your mother know you're nothing? I bet she does! *(She begins to collect her garbage, muttering to herself.)* But *they* don't know! No they don't! Their chances for survival are *zilch!* This world ain't long for this world. You wanna see a drop in temperature? You wanna see the mercury fall right through the bottom? This is only the *beginning,* Mister Weatherman!

(She has collected some but not all of her garbage, and sits again, huddled next to the garbage cans. BUDDY *enters, dressed in the rags of his clone-clown clothes, and shivering. He scampers up to the garbage cans like a hunted beast, and begins pawing through the garbage ravenously, looking for something to eat. He does not notice the* BAG LADY. *The door to the restaurant opens, with a burst of warm light and disco music, and* BRETT *and his* DATE *come out, laughing and bundled warmly. As soon as the door opens,* BUDDY *hides behind the garbage cans, frightened, and watches* BRETT.*)*

BRETT: *(Crossing to exit)* Shit, it's cold. Colder than a witch's tit!

(They exit. BUDDY *comes out from hiding, and resumes searching through the garbage. When the* BAG LADY *begins muttering he is startled.)*

BAG LADY: *(Muttering at the departing couple)* Add a disco beat to *that,* you fags! Put *that* to a heartbeat! *(To* BUDDY*)* Here, Buddy. Come sit next to me and let's keep each other warm. We'll die tonight, we'll freeze clean through to ice, but let's make our last moments together a warm occasion.

BUDDY: *(Not approaching)* I'm hungry.

BAG LADY: *(Reaches into her coat pocket and takes from it a mashed piece of cake wrapped in paper)* Here. Have some of this. It's Christmas cake from Party Cake.

BUDDY: *(Approaching and taking the cake)* Thank you.

BAG LADY: It's not bad, but it could be better. Come, sit by me.

BUDDY: *(Huddles up next to her and munches)* It's real good.

BAG LADY: Hunger makes real good. It can do that, you know. *(She takes out a bottle.)* Here, have some of this. It's plum wine, from the summer lands. It'll do your heart good.

BUDDY: *(Taking the bottle)* Thanks. *(Drinks)* That's good too.

BAG LADY: It's sweet, isn't it?

BUDDY: Yeah.

BAG LADY: Have some more. It'll make you lose body heat. Your heart's blood will rush out to fill your little frozen capillaries, and speed things along here.

(BUDDY *drinks and offers the* BAG LADY *the bottle.)*

BAG LADY: Thanks. *(Drinks)* Feeling warmer?

BUDDY: Oh yeah.

BAG LADY: Ya like it?

BUDDY: Yeah.

BAG LADY: Have some more.

(She hands him the bottle and he drinks. They sit for a bit, and then BUDDY *hands the bottle back and she drinks.)*

BAG LADY: Want the last little bit?

BUDDY: No, thanks. You finish it.

(The BAG LADY *finishes off the bottle, and then tucks it into the garbage can next to her.)*

BUDDY: I like you. You're kind.

BAG LADY: Well, that's all we got, now, ain't it?

BUDDY: You know that guy? Went by just now?

BAG LADY: Yeah?

BUDDY: I knew him once. He wasn't bad.

BAG LADY: But could be better, like Party Cake. But I bet you thought he was real good.

BUDDY: Yeah.

BAG LADY: Hunger makes real good. Do you have a hungry heart, Buddy?

BUDDY: I don't know. It's a dog's heart. Jon once told me that.

BAG LADY: Did you ever find Jon again?

BUDDY: No. By the time I found his apartment again, he'd gone away, and there were strange people there who told me to go away, and wouldn't tell me where he went.

BAG LADY: And Dondi? Do you ever see her?

BUDDY: She said she was wintering on the Island.

BAG LADY: The Island?

BUDDY: Rikers Island.

BAG LADY: *(Chuckling)* Dondi'll take care of herself all right.

BUDDY: Yeah.

BAG LADY: Feelin' cozy?

BUDDY: Oh yeah.

BAG LADY: Snuggle in, Buddy. It ain't so bad.

BUDDY: *(Snuggles his head down to her breast. She puts her arm around him.)* Thank you. I like you.

BAG LADY: I'll tell you a story, okay?

BUDDY: Okay.

BAG LADY: *(With a touch of Billie Burke)* It's a dream I once had, the most beautiful dream I ever, ever had, maybe the most beautiful dream in the whole world. Wanna hear it?

(BUDDY does not answer.)

BAG LADY: *(Her voice suddenly changes to bitter and tough.)* Well, you're gonna hear it whether you like it or not. *(Billie Burke again)* The only bad thing about this beautiful dream I had was that it ever ended. I could have gone on dreaming forever and ever, forever and ever, forever...and...ever.... *(Her voice trails off.)*

(They sit huddled together, frozen. After a while a soft snow begins to fall, covering them. A warm golden glow gradually appears in the sky, becoming more and more brilliant until it is finally dazzling; it is JON, naked and glorious, holding out his arms for BUDDY.)

JON: Buddy? Buddy?

(BUDDY stirs and looks around him.)

JON: Here, Buddy.

BUDDY: *(Looks up and gives a little gasp)* Jon?

JON: Time to go, Buddy. Time to go.

BUDDY: *(Gently extricates himself from the frozen embrace of the* BAG LADY, *who falls over against the garbage cans.* BUDDY *looks up to* JON.*)* I looked all over for you, Jon.

JON: I know.

BUDDY: Jon, I love you.

JON: I know, Buddy. And I love you.

BUDDY: Can I come to you?

JON: Sure.

*(*BUDDY *ascends to* JON *and they embrace.)*

(Blackout)

END OF PLAY

JERKER
OR
THE HELPING HAND

A Pornographic Elegy with Redeeming Social Value and a Hymn to the Queer Men of San Francisco in Twenty Telephone Calls, Many of Them Dirty

This play is dedicated to that Guy with the Walkman.

JERKER, OR THE HELPING HAND was first presented by Celebration Theater, Los Angeles, on 18 July 1986. The cast and creative contributors were as follows:

J R . . . . David Stebbins
BERT . . . . Joe Fraser

Director . . . . Michael Kearns
Scenic design . . . . Craig Gereau
Sound design . . . . Zacharia Love
Lighting design . . . . Michael Johnson
Stage manager . . . . .Susan Bell

CHARACTERS & SETTING

BERT: *a San Francisco faggot, aged anywhere from thirty to fifty or so; possibly older, though if he is, he is essentially youthful in appearance.*

J R: *a San Francisco faggot in his mid-thirties or early forties.*

ANOTHER SAN FRANCISCO FAGGOT

N B: San Francisco faggots are beautiful, loving, sexy men. They have facial hair, fairly often in the extravagant, fanciful styles of the Old West. Their eyes are alive, and their voices are relaxed and gentle. Their beauty transcends any considerations of age, race, body type, or traditional "good looks.")

Time: 1985

Place: San Francisco

NOTES

JERKER has the dubious distinction of being the play that launched the current phase of governmental repression of sexual art. On Labor Day, 1986, excerpts from the play were broadcast on Pacifica radio station K P F K in Los Angeles. The broadcast was heard by the Rev. Larry Poland of the Trinity Church in Redlands. Poland, aghast, reported what he had heard to the F C C. On April 16, 1987, the F C C, in its first effort at censorship since the George Carlin "seven dirty words" case in 1975, recommended that the Justice Department prosecute K P F K on criminal charges of broadcasting obscenity. The same day the F C C issued warnings to two other radio stations: to the U C Santa Barbara Station, for broadcasting the rock song "Makin' Bacon," and to a commercial station in Philadelphia, for broadcasting "shock radio" personality Howard Stern.

That K P F K came in for a much heavier penalty—indeed, an effort to put the station out of existence—is not necessarily an indication that the F C C considered the play that much more disgusting than "Makin' Bacon" or Stern, although the facts that the play is about *gay* sexual fantasies and has those sweet little touches of S/M might account for this. But it is all too likely that the government would like to quash Pacifica, as it is one of the very few remaining channels for the expression of dissent left in this country.

Well, the Justice Department refused to prosecute, as K P F K had been within the guidelines previously established by the F C C. The F C C then changed its guidelines, making them both vaguer and more stringent. The broadcast media responded with a show of chickenshit gutlessness, reminiscent of the betrayals of the fifties, and a "chilling effect" on the broadcast of sexual material took hold across the nation. This was, of course, just when simple, honest information about sex was most vitally and undeniably necessary.

So JERKER has inadvertently caused a lot of damage. The whole fucking nation is worse off, and it's quite conceivable that lives have been lost that could have been saved if vital, direct information on the spread of AIDS had been available on the broadcast media. Nobody ever died from being offended, but *prudery kills.*

I can only hope that JERKER has done and will continue to do some good, with its message of pride in gay identity and honesty about sex.
—Robert Chesley

Scene One

(There are two playing areas: BERT's *bed and* J R's *bed. Each has some sort of bedside lighting and a telephone; in addition,* BERT's *area can be lit by night-city light coming in his window, and his telephone has an answering machine. By* J R's *bed, propped against the wall, is a pair of Canadian crutches.)*

(Lights up on J R, *in bed, wearing only jockey shorts, playing with his erection with one hand while dialing a number on his phone. When* BERT's *phone rings, the window light comes up in his area, and we see him sleeping in bed, and then, startled awake, answering his phone sleepily. He does not turn on his bedside light.)*

BERT: Hello? *(Pause)* Hello?

J R: *(Low)* Hi.

BERT: Who is this? Hello?

J R: *(Stroking his cock under the covers)* How're you doing? I'm feeling pretty good.

BERT: Just going to sleep.

J R: You hard?

BERT: *(Realizing what kind of call this is, and deciding to go along with it)* Yeah. *(Lies back)* I'm hard, sort of.

J R: You touching yourself?

BERT: No.

J R: I am. Feels good.

BERT: Yeah?

J R: Yeah. Why don't you put your hand on your cock?

BERT: *(Doing so; aroused)* Okay. *(Pause)* Feels good.

J R: Good. Ya wearing anything?

BERT: No. I don't, in bed.

J R: Never wear pajamas?

BERT: Nope.

J R: Underwear?

BERT: Nope.

J R: Just skin, huh?

BERT: Yup.

J R: Feelin' your cock?

BERT: Yup.

J R: What's it like?

BERT: Gettin' hard.

J R: What's it look like? How big?

BERT: 'Bout seven inches.

J R: Yeah?

BERT: Yeah.

J R: Thick?

BERT: Pretty thick. And straight.

J R: You cut?

BERT: Yeah. You?

J R: Nope: sliding that foreskin up and back, up and back.

BERT: Sounds good.

J R: Feels good. Peelin' my head.

BERT: Yeah.

J R: So tell me about that cock of yours. Big head?

BERT: In proportion.

J R: Where's it feel best?

BERT: Right under the head.

J R: You hard?

BERT: Yup. Real hard.

J R: Okay. I want you to lick your finger and then just tickle that part of your cock for me: just that part, right under the head.

(BERT *licks his finger and puts it back under the covers, continues to play with himself.*)

J R: You just touching that part?

BERT: Yup.

J R: What's your other hand doing?

BERT: Holding my balls.

J R: Feel good?

BERT: Yup.

J R: I like thinking about your cock.

BERT: Yeah?

J R: I like thinking about you jerking it.

BERT: Yeah?

J R: Making it feel good.

BERT: Yeah. Yeah.

J R: How do you do it? Jack off.

BERT: How?

J R: I want you to tell me exactly what you're doing to yourself.

BERT: I'm lying back, halfway. Got my hands under the covers, and I'm holding the phone with my chin, against my pillow.

J R: Your legs straight out?

BERT: Yeah, straight out, but apart. Feet about two feet apart.

J R: Yeah?

BERT: Yeah. Got my balls in my left hand, and I'm pushin' them down between my legs, so's to pull my cockskin tight from the base. (*Licks finger again*) And my right hand's doin' just what you told me to do, just stroking that place under the head of my cock, real light.

J R: Yeah? Well, I want you to jerk it now, and I want you to tell me just exactly what you're doing, just how you do it.

BERT: Easing on my balls, now, still got 'em cupped in my hand, but I'm hooking my thumb over the base of my cock, and holding it there, firm'n hard; and I'm pressing the base, the root, you know? And now I got my other fingers on my cock—my right hand, I mean; four fingers on the underside of the shaft, thumb on top, near the head, and I'm pulling up and down, up and down, stretching my legs out and tensing, gonna shoot a load onto my belly—

(*During the end of the above speech, J R cums quietly but not silently, and then drops the phone receiver back in the cradle.*)

(*Blackout*)

Scene Two

(Lights up on both areas. J R is dialing; BERT *is reading in bed with his bedside light on when his phone rings.)*

BERT: *(Answering his phone)* Hello?

J R: *(Low and sexy)* You feelin' horny?

BERT: I could.

J R: What'ya doin'? Not asleep?

BERT: Reading.

J R: In bed?

BERT: Yeah.

J R: Not wearing anything?

BERT: Nope.

J R: You got any jockey shorts?

BERT: In my drawer.

J R: No dirty ones?

BERT: Nope.

J R: In the laundry?

BERT: Sorry.

J R: So'm I. *(Slight pause)* But the clean ones'll do.

BERT: What d'ya want me to do?

J R: I want ya to go get 'em. Will you do that?

BERT: Sure.

J R: Wait: Just get 'em. Don't put 'em on yet.

BERT: Okay. Hold a sec. *(Puts receiver down, gets out of bed and goes off; returns with a pair of jockey shorts, gets into bed again and picks up the receiver.)* Okay.

J R: You got your jockey shorts?

BERT: Yeah.

J R: I want you to smell them.

*(*BERT *does so.)*

J R: You smellin' them?

BERT: Yeah.

J R: What's it like?

BERT: Smells clean, soft.

J R: Ya like it?

BERT: Yeah.

J R: Okay. You in bed again?

BERT: Yeah.

J R: Under the covers?

BERT: Yeah.

J R: I want you to pull your jockeys on. Under the covers. Slowly. You do that for me? I'll tell you just how.

BERT: Okay. *(Starts doing so, with a bit of awkwardness, as he's also holding the phone receiver with his chin. As he does it :)*

J R: First the right foot...then the left...

BERT: Yeah.

J R: Okay, now pull them up slowly, over the calves, up to your knees. Okay?

BERT: Okay.

J R: Leave 'em there. How's your cock doin'?

BERT: Gettin' hard.

J R: Good. Play with it a bit.

(BERT does so.)

J R: Feel good?

BERT: Yeah.

J R: Good. Yeah. Now I want you to pull your jockey shorts up all the way, over your butt, over your cock.

(BERT does so.)

J R: You like the feel of that?

BERT: Yeah.

J R: You feeling your cock through your jockey shorts?

BERT: Yeah. Feels good.

J R: Real hard, huh? Pressed in there?

BERT: Yeah. Got a wet spot at the tip.

J R: Well, good! Just like a horny kid, huh? Ever wear your jockeys to bed when you were a kid, huh?

BERT: Yeah.

J R: Like the feel of getting hard in your jockeys, all snug and soft?

BERT: Yeah.

J R: Cock pressed tight? Wanna burst out?

BERT: Yeah.

J R: Let's say we're two kids in bed together, feelin' good.

BERT: Okay.

J R: Feelin' our hard-ons, in our jockeys. Snuggling.

BERT: Yeah. Good.

J R: Think you can bring yourself off? In your jockeys?

BERT: Yeah.

J R: Wanna do that for me?

BERT: Sure.

J R: I'll do mine too. I wanna listen to you.

(BERT *props the phone receiver under his chin to use both hands under the covers.*)

BERT: Two kids, huh? Two horny kids playing in bed, huh? Huh?

J R: Yeah.

BERT: Feelin' *so* good, so damn good, playin' with our cocks. Yeah, yeah. You're my little brother, huh? You're my little brother, and I'm gonna teach you how to feel good, how to feel *real* good. But we gotta be quiet, real quiet, 'cause we don't wanna get caught. Two horny brothers, gettin' it on in bed together, yeah. Yeah. *(Louder)* Hey! You my little brother? *(On the verge of cumming)* Huh? Huh?

J R: *(Also about to cum)* Yeah. Yeah! You're my big brother, look up to you!

(*They both cum, both rather quietly.* BERT *pants a bit;* J R *giggles.*)

J R: I liked that.

BERT: *(Giggling too)* Never had a brother, 'til now.

J R: Didn't either. Always wanted one. Always.

BERT: Me too.

J R: You shoot your load into your jockeys, or did you cheat?

BERT: Cheat?

J R: Take your dick out.

BERT: No—I shot in my jockeys.

J R: Good. Now you've got a dirty pair. I want you to save 'em for me. *(Hangs up)*

(Blackout)

Scene Three

(Lights up on J R dialing and on BERT's bed, which is empty, lit by the window light. BERT's phone rings two times, and is then answered by his answering machine.)

BERT: *(Voice on answering machine, with a bit of Sylvester in the background)* Hi, this is Bert. I can't come to the phone right now, but if you leave your name, your number, and the date and time of your call, I'll call you back as soon as I can. Please wait 'til you hear the beep, and please talk slowly and clearly, 'cause this machine's not doing so well, and isn't expected to make it through the summer.

(We hear a bit more Sylvester, and then the beep. J R hangs up. No blackout)

Scene Four

(Immediately following. J R is playing with himself. Then he smiles to himself— an idea has occurred to him—and lies back with his eyes closed and brings himself to the point of cumming. He sits up and re-dials, still on the verge of cumming. BERT's phone rings twice and then is answered by his machine.)

BERT: *(As before)* Hi, this is Bert. I can't come to the phone right now, but if you leave your name, your number, and the date and time of your call, I'll call you back as soon as I can. Please wait 'til you hear the beep, and please talk slowly and clearly, 'cause this machine's not doing so well, and isn't expected to make it through the summer.

(J R's timing is beautiful: just after the beep he pants two or three times, then holds for a second, and then cums with a gratifying "Ah—! Ah—!" into the receiver. He lies there for a few seconds more, then gives a low chuckle, kisses the receiver silently and sweetly, and hangs up quietly.)

(Blackout)

Scene Five

(Lights up on J R dialing and on BERT's empty bed, lit by his bedside light. BERT's phone rings a few times, and then he enters, naked and toweling himself off. He answers the phone.)

BERT: Hello?

J R: Hi there.

BERT: Hi.

J R: You want some action?

BERT: Hold a sec. Just got out of the shower. Can you call back in a minute or so?

J R: I'd rather wait.

BERT: *(Smiling)* Okay. I'll be just a minute.

J R: I'm waiting. *(And, of course, he is playing with himself.)*

(BERT puts the phone receiver on his pillow and exits. When he comes back, he has dried off, and his hair is combed. He stands for a bit, looking at the telephone receiver and playing with his cock lightly. He climbs into bed and picks up the receiver.)

BERT: You still there?

J R: Waitin' for you, Bert.

BERT: *(Smiles)* Okay, little brother. I've been planning this one.

J R: What?

BERT: Thinking about you last night, waitin' to see if you'd call—

J R: Oh?

BERT: Yeah, and I got sort of carried away, planning a little outing for you, for my little brother.

J R: Yeah?

BERT: Yeah. Wanna go? Ready?

J R: Sure.

BERT: *(Settling down)* Thought we'd do a little exploring, ya know. See what the woods are like, back of our house. Maybe pretend we're scouts or something, or maybe Indians. Just for fun, just a boy's game.

J R: *(Into it)* Yeah?

BERT: Yeah. How'd you like that, huh? Going down that trail into the woods, you following me. D'ya think I know where I'm going?

J R: Hope so. I like following you. Where ya going to take me, Bert?

BERT: Oh, a place I know. 'Bout a fifteen- or twenty-minute walk, pretty deep in the woods.

J R: Yeah?

BERT: Yeah. Don't want anyone to discover us, see? I got a special game I wanna play with you, scout. Gonna put you to the test.

J R: Yeah? What kind of test?

BERT: A little endurance test. Just wait. You'll see. Now: you see that tree over there?

J R: Yeah?

BERT: Big tree, at the edge of the clearing?

J R: Yeah?

BERT: You know what I'm gonna do to you?

J R: No.

BERT: Wanna guess?

J R: *(Faking a little panic in his voice; enjoying the game immensely)* What'ya gonna do to me?

BERT: Take a look at that tree, buddy. What do you see, in the grass there? Lying in the grass by the tree?

J R: I dunno. Can't make it out.

BERT: Step closer, then. Get a better look. If you dare.

J R: Is it—rope?

BERT: Good guess, buddy. Now: guess who's gonna get tied to that tree.

J R: You're gonna tie me to that tree, huh?

BERT: Yeah. You'd like that. Put you to the test. See how much you can take. How d'you feel about that? Think you're up to it?

J R: *(With a rush)* Sort of scared inside.

BERT: You're not gonna chicken out on me?

J R: No, sir.

BERT: Good. First we're gonna blindfold you—that's why I brought my bandana. Turn around.

J R: *(Softly)* Yeah?

BERT: Yeah. There. Blindfold you so you can't see.

J R: *(Closing his eyes; playing with himself furiously)* Thank you, sir.

BERT: Okay, now. Turn back around. Back up against the tree.
Don't stumble.

J R: Yessir.

BERT: Gotta tie you up! *Uh!* Tie you up tight and secure, so you can't get
away! *Uh!* So you can't even squirm much! *Uh!* You like the feel of that,
tied to a tree in the middle of the woods?

J R: I'm scared. What'ya gonna do to me?

BERT: Yeah—I can see you're trembling, all right: don't know what's gonna
happen to you, do you? Might be anything. Might be you're pretty helpless
right now, all tied up. Might be you've let yourself in for a little torture test,
see if you can stand it. You like standing there, all tied up to that tree and
blindfolded, waiting and wondering what's gonna happen to you? You like
that?

J R: Yessir.

BERT: Supposing I loosen your belt, huh? What you gonna do if I pull your
jeans down? Supposin' I unbutton your jeans, huh? Not much you can do
about it, is there, huh?

J R: Don't do that, sir. Please don't.

BERT: Don't do what, boy?

J R: Don't pull my jeans down, sir. Please don't.

BERT: Supposin' I *want* to do it, boy?

J R: Please don't, sir. Please.

BERT: Too bad, boy. Gonna yank your jeans down, down to your knees.
Huh! Can't go further than that, 'count of the rope around your boots—

J R: No, sir! Please don't!

BERT: There you stand, yellin' like a yellow kid, tied up there against that
tree, blindfolded, and standing in your jockey shorts, right out there in the
woods. You know what I'm gonna do to you?

J R: Please don't, sir. Let me go, sir!

BERT: You can't tell what I'm gonna do, 'cause you can't see. But I'll tell
you this much: I like the look of your hard-on, pressing against the cotton
of your jockey shorts, *straining* to get out. Keeps *trying* to get out, doesn't
know how...

J R: *(Breathless)* Yeah...yeah...

BERT: Hey—don't you cum yet, buddy. You hear me?

J R: *(As before)* Yeah.

BERT: Good boy. Man, you look hot like that, tied up against that tree. I could shoot my load all over you. But I'm not gonna—yet. Gonna put you to the test, first: gonna see how much you like ball games, boy. Gonna see how much your balls can take.

J R: *(Pulling his balls as he jerks himself)* Yessir?

BERT: That's right, boy. Now, you can't see what I'm gonna do to you right now, but you know *somethin's* gonna happen when you feel me grab your jockeys and yank 'em *up.*

J R: What'ya gonna do to me? Hey, no!

BERT: Gonna cut you free from your jockeys, boy. That's why I brought my Bowie. Cut *right up* through the leg-hole—

J R: Hey, no! No! Please,no— !

BERT: —right up—*Uh!*—through the waistband—*Uh!* There! Your jockeys are half off, and your cock's nearly free, standing up at attention with your jockeys at half-mast.

J R: Yeah?

BERT: Could leave 'em that way, one leg on...

J R: Yeah?

BERT: But I've got another use for 'em. Gonna cut off the other side. *Uh!* There! You're free. Or at least your cock is free, standing out there in the fresh air real nice and hard. Gonna spit in my palm and play with its head a bit, appreciate that nice foreskin, make you squirm. But don't you cum, boy, you hear me?

J R: *(Breathless)* Yessir. I won't, sir.

BERT: Gonna take the head of that cock in my palm and *squeeze* it, let it slide into that foreskin, knead it, yank on it real gentle, drive you mad 'cause I told you: don't cum yet, little brother.

J R: *(As before)* Yeah, yeah...

BERT: Okay, boy. You feel that? Know what that is? It's your jockey shorts, or what's left of 'em. Gonna tie you up *special:* gonna tie your jockeys around your cock and balls, right at the root of your cock, gonna yank it *tight!*—make you wince! You like that?

J R: *(As before)* Yessir. I do, sir.

BERT: Okay, gotta squat down here, now, so's to get at your balls.

J R: Yessir!

BERT: Pull 'em out, stretch 'em. Nice balls for a boy. Didn't know my little brother was growing into such a hot man. I like pulling your balls. Feel good?

J R: Yes it does, sir.

BERT: Good—'cause now I'm gonna tie 'em up too, with your jockey rag, you understand? Tied tight around your big balls, stretch 'em out. There. Now I got something to yank your balls by. Hold 'em down *firm*, make 'em *ache*.

J R: *(Pleading)* No! No, sir!

BERT: But there isn't a thing you can do about it, 'cause you're tied to that tree and you're helpless. Can't even squirm much, but you sure wish you could squirm away somehow!

J R: *(Beating furiously again, knowing the climax of the game is near)* Please don't, sir! Please!

BERT: Don't you like a little ball torture, boy?

J R: I—I can't take it, sir!

BERT: *Sure* you can, boy! I'm gonna yank a little harder, just to show you!

J R: I—please!—stop!

BERT: Don't you cum yet, you little *bastard*!

J R: Please—! Please—!

BERT: *Yah!* That hurt ya? That hurt ya?

J R: Stop! Stop! No!

BERT: I'm not lettin' go!

J R: No! I'm—I'm about to—!

BERT: *Hold* it, man! You feel me pressin' up against you?

J R: Yeah!

BERT: Ya know what I'm gonna do?

J R: No—no—I—

BERT: Huh? Gonna scrape my cheek against your face—feel the stubble, huh? That's your brother, man! Gonna force your mouth open with my tongue, huh? Gonna make you *kiss* me, huh? Gonna kiss you 'cause you're so fuckin' beautiful—

J R: *(Cumming)* Hahhh!

BERT: *Kiss* you, huh? *Kiss* you, huh? *(Cumming)* Huh! Huh! Huh!

(They both lie there for a bit, panting happily.)

J R: Heyyy—!

BERT: Shall I untie you now, huh?

J R: *(Laughing)* Thanks. That was great.

BERT: *(Little laugh)* Enjoyed it myself. Shot all over the goddamned place.

J R: *(Dabbing up with his cum towel)* You're hot.

BERT: Got a hot little brother. Bet you know more than you let on, don't you? Playin' innocent with me.

(J R laughs softly.)

BERT: You been playin' around?

J R: *(Going along with the protogame)* I—I don't know what you mean....

BERT: Don't lie to me. Bet you been playin' around *somewhere*, boy—a horny kid like you? Bet I could make you 'fess up to a *lot*, a lot of messin' around.

J R: Yeah?

BERT: Yeah. Next time.

J R: Huh.

BERT: Yeah. Right now it's bedtime for you. Gonna tuck you in, give you a little kiss, ruffle your hair a bit, and put out the light.

J R: Hey: thanks. Good night.

BERT: Good night, boy. Sweet dreams. *(Hangs up)*

(Blackout)

Scene Six

(Lights up on J R, dialing. When BERT's phone rings, the window light comes up on him, lying in bed, awake. BERT answers his phone.)

BERT: Hello?

J R: *(Low)* Hi.

(Pause)

BERT: That my little brother?

J R: Yup. Wanna play?

(Pause)

BERT: Not tonight.

J R: *(Sensing that BERT is troubled)* You okay?

BERT: Yeah—just had a heavy evening, that's all.

J R: *(Gently)* Yeah?

BERT: Just—talking with a friend who's...in bad shape.

J R: *(Half muttered)* Yeah, yeah. Sorry.

BERT: But it's okay you called. Don't be sorry.

J R: Okay. I'm not sorry. Just the sound of your voice turns me on.

BERT: *(Little laugh)* Yeah?

J R: Yeah. I got a beautiful brother. I'll beat off thinking of that.

BERT: *(Little laugh)* Okay. But call back? Another time? Promise?

J R: You bet. Good night.

BERT: Good night.

(Pause. J R hangs up first, regretfully; the lights go off on his area. BERT holds onto the receiver, lost in his thoughts, until it begins beeping at him.)

BERT: Shit. *(Hangs up)*

(Blackout)

Scene Seven

(As before. When the lights come up this time, BERT has been watching television in bed, and drinking beer; he switches the television off with a remote control device, and answers his phone.)

BERT: Hello?

J R: Hi. How're you doin'?

BERT: Okay.

J R: Good. *(Suggestive tone)* Been thinkin' 'bout you.

BERT: Yeah?

J R: *(Deciding to go ahead)* Yeah. Did my laundry today, ya know?

BERT: Yeah?

J R: Waitin' for it to dry I, uh, leaned over the dryer for a bit, ya know, pressing against it 'cause it's warm? And I got hard, thinking of you, picturing my big brother, Bert. Felt good, pressin' my hard-on against the machine, the warmth.

BERT: *(Chuckles)* How'd you picture your brother?

(Pause)

J R: Oh, I *know* what you look like, Bert.

BERT: Yeah? You do?

J R: Yeah. We met.

BERT: We did?

J R: Didn't think you remembered. How'd you think I got your number?

BERT: I gave it to you?

J R: You sure did. I don't find a brother like you by just picking a name out of the phone book.

BERT: Where?

J R: *(Laughs)* You really wanna know?

BERT: Sure.

J R: How often do you give your phone number out?

BERT: Not usually, nowadays.

J R: Okay. It was at Badlands.

BERT: Oh?

J R: *(Chuckling)* You gonna tell me you never go there? Gonna tell me you *never* stand by the men's room so's you can watch the guys piss? I've seen you there since, you know. That's a bad habit you have: it's not nice to watch guys piss.

BERT: *(Laughs)* So? I think it's nice.

J R: Y'know what you deserve?

BERT: No.

J R: Next time you're a bad boy?

BERT: What?

J R: Hmm. Maybe we should.

BERT: What?

J R: Grab you and shove you into that urinal trough and piss all over you. Spread the word in the bar that the party's in the men's room: the pig's wallowing in piss, come 'n give 'm a load of hot, steaming piss. Think you'd like that?

BERT: *(Laughs)* Yeah. *(Wistfully)* Once, once upon a time, days gone by.

J R: Oh, it's safe to get pissed *on*, Bert. Probably.

BERT: *(Seriously)* Don't know if I could control myself.

J R: *(Black English)* Shut yo mouth, chile. *(Own voice)* Pun intended.

BERT: Hmm.

(Pause)

J R: *(Resuming the game)* But you *deserve* it, for being naughty. For public *lewdness.*

(They both laugh; both are playing with themselves.)

BERT: So I gave you my number.

J R: And don't remember doing it.

BERT: Remind me.

J R: *Just* the number, on a scrap of paper.

BERT: I *don't* usually do that.

J R: You seemed to be feeling especially good that evening.

BERT: You remember when?

J R: Yup.

BERT: Well?

J R: February. Your birthday.

BERT: *(Recalling getting wrecked that evening; nodding his head)* Ooooh...

J R: February 14th, to be exact, in case you don't remember.

BERT: *(Laughs)* You gettin' fresh with me, boy?

J R: Nossir. Just wanna be courteous, friendly, helpful, and obedient.

BERT: *(Laughs)* So remind me who you are.

J R: I was the one wearing jockey shorts.

BERT: That's a big help. What d'you look like?

J R: Real stunner. Absolutely unforgettable.

BERT: Shut up. Tell me.

J R: Oh, sort of average, not bad looking. Dark hair, regulation moustache. Stand a bit under six feet tall, body in pretty good shape. The standard man-of-your-dreams type, just like thousands of others, Bert, baby.*

(J R's *description of himself may or may not be true in part or whole. Some of the audience will pick up on the fact that he is omitting mention of what must be the most obvious aspect of his appearance. If* J R *is played by a black or Asian actor, an additional problematic irony will arise, in the play as in our community. N B: Badlands is a racially mixed bar.)*

BERT: Must've been *something* special. I don't usually give out my number like that.

J R: So you keep saying. Hell, you'd need a social secretary! *(Camping)* "I'm sorry, Bert has his hands *full* right now. Can I put you on *hold?*"

BERT: *(Laughs)* So's that all the information you're gonna give me?

J R: That's all you'll ever know.

BERT: What about a name? I've gotta call my little brother something.

J R: You can call me J R.

BERT: J R.

J R: Yeah.

(Pause)

BERT: *(Switching gears; erotic)* So what'ya been up to, J R? My little brother been gettin' into trouble?

J R: *(Immediately picking up on* BERT's *tone)* I didn't do nothin'.

BERT: Yeah? What's that sticky stuff on your jockey shorts, then?

J R: *(Guilty)* I dunno.

BERT: You been playin' with yourself?

J R: *(He is, of course.)* No...

BERT: That's good, 'cause if I ever catch you doin' that, I'm gonna have to take you out to the woodshed, you understand?

J R: I...I...it's nothin'. Okay? Just forget about it.

BERT: You sound guilty as all hell, boy. Maybe I'd better take a closer look. Pull your jeans down, J R.

J R: No, I—I don'wanna.

BERT: 'Cause if I find you've been lying to me—

J R: Hey! Leggo-a-me! *Leggo!*

BERT: Lyin' to me about playing with yourself—

J R: I *didn't!* I *didn't!*

BERT: Yeah? Well, what's that, then, huh? Sticky and cold, huh? Smells like cum, boy, smells like boy-cum—

J R: No!

BERT: You shot your cum in your jockey shorts 'cause you were playin' with yourself, and then you *lied* to me about it.

J R: No!

BERT: Gonna *tan* your *ass*, J R.

J R: *(Really excited)* No! I didn't mean to!

BERT: Didn't mean to *lie* to me? Don't sass me, boy! Don't you tell me no!

J R: I'm sorry, sir.

BERT: Not as sorry as you're *gonna* be, boy! I'll give you ten counts to get to that woodshed and get your pants down to your ankles. You understand?

J R: Yessir!

BERT: One!...Two!...

J R: I'm trying, sir! Please don't!

BERT: Three!...Four!

J R: Please!

BERT: Five!...Six!...You gettin' *ready*, boy?

J R: Please don't, sir!

BERT: Seven!

J R: I said I was sorry!

BERT: Eight!

J R: *(Close)* Please! Please!

BERT: Nine!

J R: *(Cumming)* No! Nooo!

BERT: *(Over* J R's *"Nooo!")* Ten! You *ready*, boy?

*(*J R *doesn't answer; he is panting.)*

BERT: Hey, boy! You *ready*?

J R: *(Chuckling; panting)* Hey—uh—Bert, I—uh—shot. *(Laughs)*

BERT: You *what*?

J R: I shot.

(Pause)

BERT: Bad boy.

J R: It's *your* fault. You *made* me do it. *(Chuckles; dabs himself with his cum towel)*

BERT: I've half a mind to beat your ass anyway, boy. *(Sexy)* Yeah: you deserve that.

J R: *(Picking up on the possibility that* BERT *is near cumming himself)* Yeah? But—I'm sorry...I didn't mean to....

BERT: *(Bringing himself off intensely)* Yeah? Strap you up and whip your ass, boy. Gonna make you holler! Tan your ass so good you won't be able to sit down for a *week*!

J R: *(Into it; protesting, almost whimpering)* No! No!

BERT: *(Cumming)* Ah—yeah! *Yeah! Ahhh...* (Pause. He chuckles.)*

J R: *(Chuckles)* Heyyy...

BERT: Yeah?

J R: Nothin' *(Longish pause. Affectionately)* Good night, Bert.

BERT: *(Chuckles)* Good night, J R. You be a good boy, now, you hear?

J R: Yessir.

(Pause. They both are smiling, feeling their connection. They hang up.)

(Blackout)

Scene Eight

(As before. When the lights come up, BERT's area is lit by the window light, and he is in bed, crying. When his phone rings, he sits up and turns on the light, and pauses, looking at the telephone. After four rings, his machine clicks on and begins its spiel, but BERT changes his mind suddenly and answers.)

BERT: *(Over the spiel)* Wait a moment—I'm here. *(Turns off the machine)* That you, J R?

J R: Yeah. Hi. Wanna play?

(Pause)

BERT: Not tonight. Okay?

J R: Okay. *(Pause)* You okay, brother?

BERT: Yeah. Well, not really. But I'll be okay.

J R: You sure?

BERT: Yeah, thanks.

(Pause)

J R: Well...good night, then. I want you to know I really like my big brother.

BERT: *(Smiles)* I like you too, J R. Good night.

J R: 'Night.

(Pause. J R hangs up and sits thinking. BERT turns off his light and lies down. No blackout)

Scene Nine

(Immediately following. J R *re-dials and* BERT's *phone rings.* BERT *answers his phone, but does not turn on his light.)*

J R: Hey...you wanna talk? I mean, just talk?

(Pause)

BERT: Yeah. *(Pause)* Yeah, I do.

J R: What is it, huh?

BERT: *(Bursting into tears silently)* It's...I...a friend, he's in the... *(Choking)* ...in the hospital, and...

(Pause)

J R: Is it...?

(Pause)

BERT: *(Tense sigh)* Yeah. *(Pause)* They...got him on the...on the respirator....

J R: Oh. Yeah.

BERT: And he's...not gonna make it.

J R: I'm sorry.

BERT: *(Shaking with sobs)* He's...I've never...I've never seen anything so...he's... he's...Shit! He's so thin I didn't recognize him, and that fucking machine, it's like pumping him up and down, it's...*obscene.* He's...awful, he's sweating, his skin's...like *clay...*

J R: Yeah. *(Bites his lip)* Yeah, yeah. I know.

BERT: *(Collecting himself a bit)* I've never...*(Sighs tensely)* He's such a beautiful guy...he *was*...oh shit, *shit!*

J R: I wish I could hold you, put my arms around you, you know?

BERT: Yeah, I wish you could, too.

J R: Let you nestle your head into my arms, against my chest.

BERT: Yeah.

J R: Let you cry.

BERT: I'd...like that.

J R: It's so fucking hard, so fucking hard.

(Pause)

BERT: Look...I want to tell you, okay? I want to tell you about this guy, I mean: I mean the way he *was*, 'cause he was a beautiful guy. Is that okay?

J R: Sure. I'd like to hear. Tell me.

BERT: He's...okay, well his name is David, and I guess all I really have to say about him is...he's a *decent guy*. And beautiful, too, you know—not because he was any movie-idol type, not because he was a muscle builder or anything, but...because it was like there was a light inside him which made him strong, gentle...kind. *That* kind of beauty, you know: sexy, sure— sexy as anything, but *more*, too, and *all together.*

J R: Yeah?

BERT: Yeah, and...well, like I said: decent. *Nobody* deserves what—what he's going through, I know, nobody. But...! It just makes me *sick*, inside, because it's so fucking *unfair*! He came to San Francisco—you really want to hear this?

J R: Sure. If you want to tell me.

(Pause)

BERT: I do. He...well, like a *lot* of other guys, he left the Midwest. I know it's a joke, people put down the Castro for being Midwest, but it *isn't*, really: it *isn't a joke.* Okay, so David cuts hair, and I know that's a joke, too, a cliché— but he set himself up in business and he did well enough for himself, and that's not a joke either: he had to fight to have his own life the way he wanted it. That's how I knew him first, see, he cut my hair, and, well, sure... he *did* a *lot* of his customers, of course, right there in the barber's chair. He was a hot guy, and...lots of fun and...sweet, beautiful. And horny. *(Nearly in tears)* And fuck it all, *there's nothing wrong with that!*

J R: I didn't say there was.

BERT: Yeah, I know—no you didn't. But, you know, everyone's putting it down nowadays. *(Mimicking)* "The party's over! The party's over!" *(Own voice)* Well, fuck it all, no! *That wasn't just a party!* It was more, a *lot* more, at least to some of us, and it was *connected* to other parts of our lives, *deep* parts, *deep* connections. I'm not gonna deny that drugs were part of it, and I *know* for some guys it was—or it turned out to be—hell. But that's not the whole story. For me, for a *lot* of guys, it was...*living*; and it was *loving*. Yeah: *It was loving*, even if you didn't know whose cock it was in the dark, or whose asshole you were sucking. And *I don't regret a single moment of it: not one.*

(Pause)

J R: Yeah.

(Pause)

BERT: I'm not sorry.

(Pause)

J R: Bert?

BERT: Yeah?

(Pause)

J R: I was in Vietnam. I don't want to talk about that now, except to say I nearly died there. And for what? What would have been the purpose? Greed, stupidity: that's what I gave...a part of my life for. And some of the things I saw there: I still see them sometimes when I close my eyes: like they were so terrible, so *evil*, they burned into my eyes and I'll see them as long as I live. I'm not going to tell you about them. I don't tell anyone. But take my word.

BERT: Yeah.

J R: I just wanna say: I know, I *saw* what..."immoral" means, I learned what "immoral" means. And that's why nobody but nobody tells me I'm immoral if I love a man, if I love a hundred men in one night: if I love sucking ass, if I love licking boots, if I love taking piss from a guy's cock, or if I have a quickie blow job in the Union Square men's room; all that is *good*—really, truly, *basically* good. Something in me *knows* that, knows that it's just the exact opposite of the evil I've seen.

(Pause)

BERT: Yeah.

J R: But now I'm scared.

BERT: Yeah.

J R: And you're scared.

BERT: Yeah. Yeah, I am.

(Pause)

J R: A friend was telling me yesterday: when he beats off? He fantasizes it's four or five years ago, *before*...He can't even *fantasize* he's doing what he wants to do with another man unless it's before...all this.

BERT: Yeah. I understand.

J R: He's scared, too.

BERT: Yeah.

J R: So what does that leave us, huh? Not much.

BERT: No.

(Pause)

J R: Not much, except what's maybe best, and what *can't* be destroyed: caring for each other. Even if we're... *(Long pause)* doomed. Loving can't be killed: it's stronger. That's why even if I *can't* hold you in my arms, just telling you I want to...

BERT: Helps. It helps me.

J R: Helps me, too.

(Pause)

BERT: You're a beautiful guy.

J R: *(Pause)* Maybe we're the lucky ones.

BERT: Maybe.

(Pause)

J R: You all right now?

BERT: Better. Thanks.

(Pause)

J R: Thank you for telling me about David.

BERT: Yeah.

J R: Good night, brother.

BERT: Good night. *(Slight pause. He hangs up, and the lights in his area go out as he snuggles down into bed.)*

J R: *(Eyes closed, head raised, clutching the telephone receiver; bitterly)* Yeah. I'm beautiful. I'm one of the lucky ones. I didn't have my face blasted away.

(Pause. J R hangs up.)

(Blackout)

Scene Ten

(As before. Window light on BERT's area; another man is with him in bed, dozing. BERT answers his phone immediately, and talks quietly.)

BERT: J R?

J R: Yeah. Hi.

BERT: Hi.

J R: How're you doing?

BERT: I'm okay?

(Pause)

J R: And...David?

BERT: He's okay, too. Now.

(Pause)

J R: Yeah.

(Pause)

BERT: Thanks for calling. Thanks for asking.

J R: I'm sorry.

BERT: We're all in this together. No use being sorry.

J R: Yeah. I know.

BERT: But...it's good to hear your voice. Thanks, really.

J R: Kisses and hugs. *(Kisses the receiver silently)*

BERT: Same to you, buddy.

J R: Good night.

BERT: Gimme a call tomorrow, okay? Can you?

J R: Sure.

BERT: Thanks.

(J R *kisses the receiver again and hangs up.*)

(Blackout)

Scene Eleven

(As before. BERT *is reading a porn magazine and playing with himself. When the phone rings, he takes a final toke on the joint he has been smoking, and then answers the phone; as he talks he holds the receiver by his chin while he pinches out the end of the roach.)*

BERT: 'Lo—J R?

J R: Yeah. How're you doing?

BERT: 'T's okay.

J R: Wanna play?

BERT: Wanna talk. For a bit. 'T's okay? Then maybe play.

J R: Sure.

BERT: Don't mean heavy talk. Just I like hearing your voice, and I want to feel good, talk about good stuff.

J R: *(Laughs)* What do you mean?

BERT: I wanna know more about you.

J R: You sure?

BERT: Yeah.

J R: Like what?

BERT: Like what does the J R stand for?

J R: James Reilly.

BERT: That your whole name?

J R: No. First and middle.

BERT: You're not going to tell me more?

J R: No.

BERT: Why not?

J R: I like anonymous encounters.

BERT: This is getting to be more than an encounter, J R.

J R: *(Laughs)* A friend of mine, you know—I kid you not—he's had an ongoing anonymous encounter with a guy for *fifteen years* now. A long-term relationship, see, but a relationship between strangers. A guy he cruised on the tram—the old, green blimps? Well, he'd been cruising this guy, mornings and evenings, to and from work, for months and months, maybe even a year. Until the inevitable happened: MUNI broke down in the tunnel, the car was jam-packed, this guy was standing pressed against my friend, who was seated, you see, and well, you can imagine the rest. The next week the guy followed my friend home, got his address and name from the mailbox—so I guess it isn't *entirely* anonymous after all, not *quite*—and called him up, asked if he could come over. My friend said sure. And they've been going at it for fifteen years now. But they've never said a word to each other, *not a word*, except over the phone, and that's just the bare minimum: yes or no.

BERT: *(Amused)* Ha!

J R: An anonymous relationship. They don't know anything about each other.

BERT: I love it. It's—San Francisco.

J R: *(Laughs)* Yup. And *nobody* can say it's without meaning: just that both parties have voluntarily chosen to limit the *medium* for meaning—limit it to what's good, limit it to sex. At least I think we can *assume* it's good, after fifteen years.

BERT: *(Laughs)* I guess so. So you're not telling me your last name?

J R: Why should I? What's it to you?

BERT: Well, tell me just a bit more about yourself.

J R: *(Calculatingly)* I will, if *you* tell me a story.

BERT: A story?

J R: About San Francisco. And anonymous love. I'm writing a history, a history of love among strangers.

BERT: *(Laughs)* I gotta think. But you tell me first.

J R: I just did.

BERT: No, I mean more—about you. Who are you?

J R: What the hell do you mean?

BERT: You know.

J R: Well, I'm your little brother, for one thing.

BERT: I already know *that*. What...well, what do you do?

J R: About what?

BERT: Stop teasing. Who *are* you? What...work do you do?

J R: Are you a New Yorker? Don't answer.

BERT: Why?

J R: Well, just the very *idea* that a person *is* his job.

BERT: Oh, come on.

J R: All right. I'll tell you. This might surprise you, but I'm a—historian. And a liar, which is the same thing. Now that I've told you what I "am," you're free to believe what you want. I admit I've told you some lies.

BERT: But I know some things about you anyway.

J R: So tell me.

BERT: What I do?

J R: No! I don't want to know! I already know more than I want to know about *that*.

BERT: Oh? How?

J R: Well, I have the advantage—or disadvantage—of knowing, and remembering, what you look like. And so, I am sorry to say, I've seen you in a three-piece suit, coming out of the MUNI station and walking down Castro Street with that beautiful horde of guys, all obviously on their way home from nine-to-five jobs downtown. I don't want to know anything more about *that*. I prefer to think of you in your Badlands drag, or your Ambush drag—'cause I've seen you there, too.

BERT: Oh?

J R: Yeah. We pissed together there a couple of weeks ago. I thought it was a hoot. Nice dick you got.

BERT: I don't remember.

J R: Your dick? Well, its—

BERT: No, *you*.

J R: Typical, typical.

BERT: No. I don't remember who I piss with.

J R: Just their dicks, huh? You didn't exactly look me in the face.

BERT: Well, next time say hello.

J R: Not on your life. Tell me a story.

BERT: Oh...yeah.

J R: Yeah?

BERT: Well...okay. I know. This is a true story.

J R: I'll put it into my history of San Francisco. And that's the truth.

BERT: Okay.

J R: Just make it hot.

BERT: It's not kinky, just...nice.

J R: Okay. Go on. Just remember I'm playing with myself. *(He is.)*

BERT: Okay. It was quite a few years ago, I guess, because I was still living on O'Farrell Street, you know: the edge of the Tenderloin. And because I remember it was the first time I ever saw anyone wearing a Walkman. Maybe it was 1979, or around then. But anyway: it was one of our pretty, pretty afternoons—sunny, breezy, air *so* clear, you know—and I was walking down Hyde Street from the CALA at California, carrying my groceries home, and there in front of me, walking down the hill too, was a gorgeous guy, bopping to the music he was listening to on his Walkman. *Pretty* guy: Smiling eyes, full of energy and...happiness. Nice beard. Nice, hairy legs—he was wearing shorts. So I caught up with him at the corner, waiting to cross, and he caught my eye and smiled at me and took off his headphones and didn't say anything but put the headphones on me so I could hear. And we walked down the hill that way, hand-in-hand in fact, and connected by the wire from the headphones. And we were both turning on—just out of happiness, or it seems like that's what it was, now. You still with me?

J R: Yes, I am. Tell me more.

BERT: Well, I smoked a bit before you called, and I know I can get talking more than *anyone* wants to listen.

J R: This one wants to listen. Go on.

BERT: Okay. Where was I?

J R: On Hyde Street, hand-in-hand with a hunk and his Walkman.

BERT: Yeah, yeah, yeah. So...we got to O'Farrell and I turned to him and took off the headphones to hand them to him, but he said just: "Take me home. I'll give you the greatest fuck west of the Mississippi." Just that.

J R: So? Did you? Did he?

BERT: Are you kidding? This was 1979. And I was *hard*. And so was he.

J R: And?

BERT: And I took him up to my apartment and I didn't even put the groceries away: we went straight to the bedroom and stripped, and I pulled down the Murphy bed and we cuddled and played around for a bit before he started working on my ass. *(He starts playing with himself.)* He rolled me over onto my stomach and told me just to relax, and he started with a backrub, which was just heaven; then he worked his way down, of course. He was kneeling between my legs, and he worked my asshole with Lube for the longest time, getting it to relax so there was just no tightness, no fear, just letting go so that I almost dozed off, even though I was hard—like a morning dream when you don't have to wake up and get out of bed, but can just lie there and feel good. Let's see: then he lowered himself onto me and slid his cock in all the way, but so gently and smoothly—and I was so relaxed—that there was not even a bit of pain. I don't think my ass has ever felt so sensitive. His cock felt *warm* in me, and *full*, so nice and full.

(J R is close to cumming, but he is quiet about his panting as he listens.)

BERT: So he began sliding in and out of me, in and out so gently! —so gently! And he kissed me behind the ear and he sucked my shoulder, and we both sort of giggled because we were feeling so good together. He was right, absolutely right: I've never had such a gentle, *sensitive* fuck, before or after, and he must have gone at it twenty minutes at the *very* least, just sliding his cock back and forth so steadily inside my ass, and both of us on the edge of cumming, but not tensing up to it, but relaxing instead, you know, and letting the feeling, the tingle, go through all of our bodies, and feeling so good to be so close, body to body. And then he whispered in my ear: "You're gonna feel me cum inside you" —and I did: I felt his cum pulse up his shaft inside my ass, I could count the pulses—

(J R cums silently.)

BERT: — and it felt warm and good, one of the most wonderful things I think I've ever felt, one of the most wonderful *connections* I think I've ever had with another person, one of the most beautiful acts of love I think I have ever known. And then we rolled over onto our sides, and he was still in me, we just lay there for a bit. And that was all: we kissed and hugged and said goodbye, and for the rest of the day and all that evening I *glowed*, I just *glowed*, like he was still making love to me.

J R: Woooo...that was *nice*. *(Dabs himself off)*

BERT: You liked that?

J R: I came.

BERT: *(Laughs)* Really?

J R: Would I lie to you? Of *course* I did.

BERT: Well, I know it's possible to get a good fuck anywhere in the world—I guess it is, or used to be. But there was something about the...*happiness* of this guy, the happiness, and the...easy, open clean *naturalness* of the whole thing, that makes the story—San Francisco, for me.

J R: I agree. Absolutely.

BERT: *And it was love*, even if it was only for a few hours.

J R: Which is frequently best.

BERT: Yup. *(Laughs. Pause)* Hey, thanks.

J R: For what?

BERT: For reminding me.

J R: Of what?

BERT: No: For getting me to remember—that it was love. And...a virus can't change that: can't change that fact.

(Pause)

J R: No, it can't.

(Pause)

BERT: Thanks. Really.

J R: Kisses and hugs, brother.

BERT: *(Little laugh)* Same to you. *(Softly)* Hey...good night.

J R: Thanks for the story, Bert. *(Pause)* Good night. *(Kisses the telephone receiver silently and hangs up.)*

(Blackout)

Scene Twelve

(As before. BERT is lit by window light, but puts his bedside light on when he answers his phone.)

BERT: 'Lo. That you, J R?

J R: Yeah. What's up? Pun intended.

BERT: Not doin' so well.

J R: Oh?

BERT: Flu or something. Been in bed all day, feeling rotten. *(He coughs into his pillow.)*

J R: I'm sorry. You gonna be okay?

BERT: Oh yeah, yeah. I never get sick for long.

J R: Good. *(Pause)* Wanna talk?

BERT: Yeah. Can't get to sleep anyway, feeling sorry for myself. I'm a bad patient, I complain, so— *(Breaks off to cough into his pillow)*

J R: You sure you're okay?

BERT: Yeah. Get my mind off it, I'll be okay. More than okay. Tell me a story.

J R: A story?

BERT: Yeah. A bedtime story.

J R: Like a fairy tale?

BERT: Yeah, but just the happy ending, okay?

J R: Hmmm.

BERT: Will you?

J R: I'm thinking. Give me a bit.

BERT: Okay. I — *(Coughs into his pillow)*

J R: What?

(Pause, while BERT coughs. Then:)

BERT: Nothin', it's nothing. I was just going to say it doesn't have to be a dirty story...

J R: Pigs in mud?

BERT: You know. Just a bedtime story, not a playtime story. I just wanna lie here and listen to you, 'cause I've been alone all day.

J R: Okay. I know. This is a fantasy I used to have—to enjoy, love it—when I was a kid. For years it was my favorite fantasy, and maybe it was my first fantasy, or maybe it was a dream I had to begin with. Okay?

BERT: Sure.

J R: I've never told it to anyone before.

BERT: Yeah? Good. Then it'll be *our* fantasy, just ours.

J R: Okay, sounds good to me. So... *(An idea)* ...yeah! We'll do it *together*, so that at the end there'll be not just two of us, but *three*.

BERT: What?

J R: You'll see...yeah. It'll work. But—uh.

BERT: Yeah.

J R: Okay, I'll just say this: when I was a kid, I didn't know what men *did* together—I mean sexually. I *really, really* wanted to *touch* men, *be* with them, smell them, be in bed together...I guess it was the *affection* I wanted. And you know? I think that's still basically it, still what I want the most.

BERT: Yeah?

J R: Yeah, well, we *are* being intimate here, *aren't we*? What I'm trying to say is that when I was a kid that's as far as I got in my fantasies: just into bed, because I didn't *know* there was sex, didn't know it consciously. So this is an *affectional* fantasy, but not exactly a *sexual* fantasy. See?

BERT: That's okay. That's fine with me.

J R: Okay. Here goes then. Let's see. How to start.

(Pause. A change of lighting and perhaps a music cue indicate that "real" time and space have dissolved, and what we now see is fantasy. J R puts his phone receiver down and stands by his bed—without his crutches. During the rest of this sequence he talks directly to BERT, *though* BERT *continues to talk only to his phone receiver; as he tells his story, J R, "invisible" to* BERT, *eventually moves into* BERT's *area, and sits on* BERT's *bed, like an adult telling a child a bedtime story.)*

J R: Let's pretend I'm standing by your bed, okay?

BERT: Okay.

J R: And I put out my hand to you, and you take it, and you get out of bed.

BERT: Yeah.

J R: And I undress you.

BERT: I *am* undressed.

J R: Pretend you're wearing pajamas, okay? I want to undress you.

BERT: Okay.

J R: So...I unbutton your pajama jacket and let it slip to the floor, and I pull down your pajama bottoms and you step out of them so you're standing naked.

BERT: Yeah, okay.

J R: Then I get undressed, too, so we're both naked. And I tell you not to be afraid: don't be afraid of anything.

BERT: Okay.

J R: 'Cause I'm taking you to the front door, okay? And we're going to go out, naked, okay? Don't be afraid. I'm holding your hand.

BERT: Okay.

J R: So: I—no, *you*: you open the door, and there, in front of us, is a beautiful, enchanted forest. Uh—this isn't your standard *Drummer* fantasy, you understand.

BERT: Go ahead. I love it.

(Two or three times during the course of the ensuing story BERT *coughs into his pillow.)*

J R: Okay. So...well, okay, when I was a kid I called this forest the Forbidden Forest. It's filled with terrible perils and frightful things. But we're going to go to the end of the story: all the adventures and battles and scary things are over now, done with. We're—*two* young princes, fairy-tale princes, brothers, and we're walking through the beautiful forest. It's near nightfall. The last bit of the sun hits the top of the trees, and a sudden cool breeze comes through the forest, touches our faces and combs through our hair. We're weary, terribly weary, but we have only a little bit further to go. And then there, in front of us, in the very middle of the Forbidden Forest, stands a beautiful palace, all made of smooth black marble, polished like mirror. It's very dim and looming in the dusk. The gates of the palace open magically when we approach, and we walk first through a luxuriant garden. The grand doors of the palace open before us, and we enter a great hall, lit by torches. As we walk in, torches set in the walls light up before us and are extinguished as we pass. We are being led up a black marble staircase and then down a high, gloomy hall to a chamber where a large, steaming bath has been prepared for us. We take off our clothes, and—

BERT: I thought we were naked.

J R: Oh—no, no. When we became princes we got princes' clothing, like Prince Charming. I always was more interested in *him* than in the fairy-tale princesses—Snow White, Cinderella, whatever. I identified with Sleeping *Beauty*: I wanted that kiss.

*(*BERT *laughs.)*

J R: You enjoying this?

BERT: *(Perhaps a bit surprised that he is; nodding)* Yeah.

J R: Okay. I'll go on. We...take off our clothes and bathe. We wash each other. And the water takes away our weariness and leaves us...light, and content. And when we get out of the bath, there are fresh clothes put out for us, and we dress each other. And a strange, distant music—very sweet, very pure—calls us back down the high gloomy hall and down the black marble stairs to the banquet hall. It, too, is lit by torchlight, and there are three places set at the huge, old table—set for a plain supper of clear, steaming broth and fresh bread, and red wine in golden goblets. We take our seats across from each other, knowing we are to wait for the appearance of our host, and it turns out that he has been the music that we heard: the sweet, gentle music...coalesces, comes together and becomes visible at the head of the table, and there he stands, a beautiful man, without age, smiling. And when we see him, the last bit of fear we had in all our wonder just melts away, and we know we are safe at last, and that his magic is good. And as we take our supper we tell him of all our adventures and perils and...*bitter* sorrows we had journeying through the Forbidden Forest, to find his palace; and he questions us about each adventure, peril, and sorrow, and from the answers he brings forth from us we understand that each one, even the most terrible, was a lesson on our journey to the palace; and we understand that we ourselves were lessons for others whose paths crossed ours in the Forest. And when all is over and all is told, it is late, and we, the three of us, rise from the table and ascend the spiral staircase, round and round, up a tower. He leads us, holding a torch. And at the top of the tower is the bedchamber, with a large, old royal bed. The three of us undress and part the bedcurtains and lie down together in each others' arms—we three beautiful men, two princely brothers and a man made of magic and music. We hold each other and we kiss...

(J R *leans over* BERT *and kisses him;* BERT *still relates only to his telephone receiver.)*

J R: ... and we drift off to sleep. *(Long pause)* And that's all.

(J R *returns to his bed and picks up his telephone receiver; the lighting indicates a return to "real" time and space. [Michael Kearns deserves credit for the idea of having* J R *arise from his bed, cross into* BERT's *area, and kiss him.])*

J R: That's the happy ending.

BERT: Sleep?

J R: Yeah.

BERT: Sounds good to me.

J R: *(Lightening)* Oh, in the morning we get up and run through the woods naked, bathe in the crystal spring, pluck golden pears in the magic garden—that sort of thing.

BERT: *(Laughs)* Sounds great. *(Pause)* It's been such a *long* time since anyone told me a bedtime story. Not since I was a kid. *(Coughs into his pillow)* Thank you.

J R: Not too unbutch for you?

BERT: No, I loved it.

J R: Good. *(Little laugh. Pause)* Think you'll be able to get to sleep now?

BERT: Yeah. I think so. *(Coughs into his pillow)* Call again soon, huh?

(Pause)

J R: *(Regretfully)* I'm going to be out of town for a week or so.

BERT: *(Disappointed)* Yeah?

J R: Yeah. Sorry. Work. New York.

BERT: Ugh.

J R: Well, I'll give you a call, just to see how you're doing.

BERT: Thanks. I'm not an invalid, you know.

J R: I didn't mean that. Maybe I'll call just because I'm horny for you, okay?

BERT: *(Laughs)* Okay.

J R: And I can tell you, you better get yourself ready for some brother-to-brother, sweaty, down-and-dirty *pig* sex, you understand?

BERT: Yeah?

J R: Enough of this nicey-nice-lovey-dovey stuff: I'm gonna make you eat ass and suck my balls and drink my piss like you never have before, you get me?

BERT: Hot, throbbing cocks? Hard, pounding muscles?

J R: You got it. Meanwhile, you can work on those jockey shorts you started for me; get 'em real stiff and crusty for me, okay? I wanna dream about that when I'm in New York.

BERT: Okay.

J R: Okay. Good night. *(Kisses the receiver silently)*

BERT: Good night.

(They hang up.)

(Blackout)

Scene Thirteen

(BERT's *phone rings. The window light comes up in his area;* J R's *area remains in darkness.* BERT's *bed is empty. We hear his machine answer the call: mellow music, and then* BERT's *voice, sounding a bit drunk and/or stoned, saying* "Good evening— or good whatever time of day it is you're calling, though it's evening now as I record this message for you, and a beautiful evening it is. An especially good evening to my little brother, if it's you calling; I'm really sorry to miss your call, if it's you, 'cause I miss you and I want you to know—" *and then a click and the beep. We then hear, coming over the machine,* J R *laughing and saying:* "I miss you, too. Sorry you're out. But I'll be home Wednesday, so sit by your phone with your cock in your hand ready, okay? Kisses and hugs." *And then we hear him hang up, and the machine clicks off.*)

Scene Fourteen

(*Lights up on* J R *in bed, playing with himself and dialing; the window light comes up on* BERT's *area, but his bed is empty. We hear his machine answer the call.*)

BERT'S ANSWERING MACHINE: (*Judy Garland singing*):
You really shouldn't have done it,
You hadn't any right.
I really shouldn't have let you
Kiss me.
And although it was wrong
I never was strong,
So as long as you've begun it,
And you know you shouldn't have done it...
Oh, do it again—

BERT: (*Voice on the answering machine*) Please leave me a message. I'll get back to you as soon as I can. Thanks.

J R: Hold, on brother. I'll call you back in a minute.

(*Hangs up. Lights out in* BERT's *area only.* J R *continues to play with himself. No blackout*)

Scene Fifteen

(Immediately following, J R *is playing with himself.)*

J R: Gonna crawl into bed with my brother. Gonna snuggle next to him, huh? Gonna feel his body next to me, gonna slide my legs right down next to his, under the sheets, huh? Gonna feel *warm* and *cozy*, next to him...yeah. *(Long, low)* Hey...I'm gettin' hard. I like being next to you, Bert, I like your warmth, huh? I like your smell, next to me, huh? Hey! What'ya doin'? Wrestlin'? *(Laughs)* Yeah! Yeah! Hey, you got me *pinned down* under you! *(Starts dialing his phone, panting)* Hey—you're not gonna...? Hey, no, you leave my jockey shorts on! Leggo! Leggo! You're not supposed to...!

(The lights do not come up on BERT's *area. Over the speaker system we hear a phone ring three or four times.)*

J R: Hey! Hey! *Stop* that! It feels too good! *Stop* it! *Stop* it!

(We hear a woman's voice answer the phone: "Hello? Hello? Who is this?" Simultaneously:)

J R: You're suckin' your brother's cock! You're gonna make me shoot! I'm gonna shoot my load right down your hot— *(Suddenly realizing he has misdialed; breaking into laughter and cumming accidentally)* Oh no! Oh shit!

(Shaking with laughter, he hangs up; still laughing, he dabs himself with his cum towel. No blackout)

Scene Sixteen

(Immediately following. J R, *still shaking with laughter, re-dials. Lights up in* BERT's *area; his bed is empty, as before.)*

BERT'S ANSWERING MACHINE: *(Judy Garland singing)*:
You really shouldn't have done it,
You hadn't any right.
I really shouldn't have let you
Kiss me.
And although it was wrong
I never was strong,
So as long as you've begun it,
And you know you shouldn't have done it...
Oh, do it again—

BERT: *(Voice on the answering machine)* Please leave me a message.
I'll get back to you as soon as I can. Thanks.

J R: *(So convulsed with laughter it's difficult to get it out)* Shit, Bert, you're never gonna believe this, but *(Breaks down into giggles)* I—I—no, I'll tell you later. I fucked it up. Good night, sweetheart. *(Hangs up)*

(Blackout)

Scene Seventeen

(Lights up on J R *dialing. The window light comes up on* BERT's *area, but his bed is empty as before.)*

BERT'S ANSWERING MACHINE: *(Judy Garland singing)*:
You really shouldn't have done it,
You hadn't any right.
I really shouldn't have let you
Kiss me.
And although it was wrong
I never was strong,
So as long as you've begun it,
And you know you shouldn't have done it...
Oh, do it again—

BERT: *(Voice on the answering machine)* Please leave me a message. I'll get back to you as soon as I can. Thanks.

J R: Just your little brother, wondering where you are. *(Hangs up; grimaces in comic puzzlement as the lights fade.)*

Scene Eighteen

(Lights up on J R *dialing. The window light comes up on* BERT's *area, but his bed is empty, as before.)*

BERT'S ANSWERING MACHINE: *(Judy Garland singing)*:
You really shouldn't have done it,
You hadn't any right.
I really shouldn't have let you
Kiss me.
And although it was wrong
I never was strong,
So as long as you've begun it,
And you know you shouldn't have done it...
Oh, do it again—

BERT: *(Voice on the answering machine)* Please leave me a message. I'll get back to you as soon as I can. Thanks.

J R: Hey, Bert—where are you? I asked Hank at the Badlands whether he'd seen you, and he said you hadn't been around for weeks. Can you—please give me a call. My number is 771-0725 *(Pause)* Thanks. *(Hangs up and sits thinking as the lights fade)*

Scene Nineteen

(Lights up on J R dialing. The window light comes up on BERT's *area, but his bed is empty, as before.)*

BERT'S ANSWERING MACHINE: *(Judy Garland singing)*:
You really shouldn't have done it,
You hadn't any right.
I really shouldn't have let you
Kiss me.
And although it was wrong
I never was strong,
So as long as you've begun it,
And you know you shouldn't have done it...
Oh, do it again—

BERT: *(Voice on the answering machine)* Please leave me a message. I'll get back to you as soon as I can. Thanks.

J R: Bert, it's J R. Look, maybe it's stupid, but I'm worried about you. Would you—please give me a call—my number is 771-0725. Okay? I just wanna know you're okay. Thanks. I...love you. Please call.

(Hangs up. Sighs tensely and chews his thumbnail and fights back tears as the light fades)

Scene Twenty

(Lights up on J R dialing. The lights do not come up on BERT's *area. Over the speaker system we hear two rings, and then a mechanical voice: "We're sorry. The number you have reached. Two. Six. Eight. Five. Four. Oh. Nine. Has been disconnected. Please check that you have dialed correctly. Two. Six. Eight—"* J R *hangs up, stunned. He sobs convulsively as the lights fade out.)*

J R: Oh no. Oh no. Oh no...

END OF PLAY

DOG PLAYS:

(WILD) PERSON, TENSE (DOG)

THE DEPLORATION OF ROVER

HOLD

These plays are dedicated to the memory of Geoff Mains.

NOTES

DOG PLAYS has won no dubious distinction as of this writing, except, perhaps, as the most unremittingly sad piece for theater since the Greeks. These odd little plays, which can, of course, be performed separately, are all that I have written for theater in the past two years, since getting the Diagnosis. In a sense, they are my first AIDS plays. The previous plays deal with the impact of AIDS on gay-identified lives and communities. But getting the diagnosis yourself thrusts you instantly out of the Golden Land of the (seemingly) Healthy, and into a different territory. These plays are from that territory.

The plays are to be performed with a set of songs by Stephen Foster, in this order:

Old Folks at Home
(WILD) PERSON, TENSE (DOG)
Gentle Annie
THE DEPLORATION OF ROVER
Old Black Joe
HOLD
My Old Kentucky Home, Good Night!

The songs must be sung in Foster's original versions, not in arrangements, or in versions altering Foster's utterly heartfelt lyrics. For the reading of DOG PLAYS in New York, the whole cast joined in singing Foster's simple four-part harmony for the chorus of *My Old Kentucky Home, Good Night!* The houselights were brought up, and the audience joined in: "Weep no more my lady..." It helped.

DOG PLAYS was first presented to the public as a staged reading by 3-Dollar Bill Theater as part of the Reading Our Minds series, at the Apple Corps Theatre in New York City, on 7 February 1990.

DOG .... Kenneth Talberth
BUCK .... Michael O'Connor
FIDO .... Barry Hoff
ROVER .... John Collis
LAD .... John Finch

Countertenor .... John Collis
Piano .... Chris DeBlasio

Director .... Nicholas Deutsch

(WILD) PERSON,
TENSE (DOG)

CHARACTERS & SETTING

DOG
BUCK

A South-of-Market leather bar, San Francisco, 1989

(In the initial darkness all that can be seen are the large red numerals of a digital clock, reading twenty-some minutes after eleven o'clock. We sit in silence for a minute or two, waiting for and watching the minutes pass. Then the lights come up gradually: fairly dim, reddish and amber bar lighting, with a few spots directed at crotch level. We are in a South-of-Market leather bar, and the spotlit crotches are those of dummies or cutouts, representing the men standing at the bar on a Saturday night. With the lights, the music comes up; it is strange and nightmarish, and too loud, with a brutal, steady, percussive beat—we immediately feel trapped by it. The beat halts intermittently for two or three bars or so, allowing us to hear distant, forlorn coyote howls, and then resumes implacably. DOG enters the bar S R. He is a forty-five-year-old San Francisco faggot, wearing some leather, sexy enough, but not out to impress anyone with a meticulous Tom-of-Finland image. He edges past some of the dummies politely, nodding at one in greeting, and then looks out at the audience; the moment he does so, the music stops abruptly.)

DOG: *(To the audience)* I've just seen a ghost. *(Long pause; he is rattled.)* But he ain't dead yet.

(Pause. The music begins again abruptly the moment DOG breaks eye contact with the audience. He turns and makes his way through the "men" to the bar, mimes getting a bottle of Calistoga water, and then returns D S to address the audience again. Again, the instant he looks out to the audience the music stops and allows the audience to breathe again. The music will not return for a while, now; DOG speaks to us in a silence which is nearly as unnerving. The director may choose to emphasize this silence with a scarcely-noticeable tick-tock.)

DOG: A ghost. But alive. A live ghost. Standing outside, just outside that door. I don't know who he is. I mean I *do* know I've seen him, but I don't know who he is. I know I've seen him, and I know where I've seen him, but I didn't ever expect to see him again. I didn't expect to see him again because the last time I saw him was, I think, a year ago, or so. A year or so ago, and at that time he didn't look like he would live this long. But there he is, still alive. I don't know how. *(Bitterly)* I don't know *why*, either. But there he is, like a ghost, whoever he is. *(Pause; sigh)* Where I've seen him—where I *used* to see him—is on Castro Street. Not that I wanted to look. But what do you do? *Do* you look? Is it cruel to look, or is it crueler *not* to look, to ignore what you don't want to look at? *(A consideration)* To ignore—not a *what*, but *someone*, a *person* you don't want to look at—? There he was, there on the sidewalk, sitting on the sidewalk. Of course he knew he was going to be looked at—or *not* looked at. Either way it's cruel. The whole fucking thing is cruel, and I'm certainly not saying he *shouldn't've* been on Castro Street, *shouldn't've* been showing himself in public. And begging. A *lot* of beggars

on Castro Street now. He was just sitting there, a bit up from Hibernia
Beach—what we used to call Hibernia Beach—this guy, this ghost,
this—*reminder*, sitting there crossed-legged on the pavement, a little
hand-lettered sign taped to the top of his open cigar box, the sign
announcing that he was—*is*—*(Pause) was*...an artist, dying. That's where
I saw him, used to see him, up until a year or so ago. And because I stopped
seeing him there, I admit I never expected to see him again. And the funny
thing is I hadn't thought about it, about him, until a day or two ago, when
for some reason he came to mind and I realized I *hadn't* seen him for that
long. And I assumed he was dead. Among the dead, among the many,
many dead. Yes, it gave me a pang. I grieved, grieved a bit for him,
even though I didn't—*don't* know who he is. And then tonight, there
he was—there he *is*, outside the door. I'm sure it's him. Our eyes met,
and I recognized him immediately, this guy I'd already grieved for, this
guy I thought must be dead. I don't think he recognized me, though. I don't
see how he could have, don't see why he should have. *(Pause)* But there was
something there in that glance, that look—even though I looked away almost
immediately...maybe he read my astonishment. There was something,
some current, though. Something happened between that—that *ghost* and
me. *(He takes a drink on his Calistoga, without breaking contact with the audience,
and waits. Then:)* Well, I can tell you: this is *not* why I came out tonight,
to get depressed, to get morbid. Not that there's much choice necessarily,
nowadays, as you probably already know: you never know when it's going
to hit you in the face, what we're going through: the horror. Hell, we face it
every day, it's just a part of our lives. Sometimes it might seem it's most of
our lives, and sometimes it is. But it *isn't* all of life, not really. There's other
stuff, good stuff. Though it can be hard to find sometimes. And I'm not sure
I'm going to find it here, tonight, standing around this bar. *(Pause)* I'm not
going to tell you what I went through today, okay? I just want to relax, get
my mind off it, feel good on a Saturday night. I wonder if I can do that?
Let's listen to the music.

*(DOG breaks contact with the audience and looks around the bar. The moment he
does so, the music returns, horrifyingly. He takes another drink from his Calistoga,
and saunters over S L, taking a stance leaning against a meatrack, perhaps to cruise
the crowd. The pounding halts for a coyote break, and during the eerie howling
BUCK enters the bar S R. BUCK is, of course, the "ghost" DOG has seen outside
the bar. It is up to the director how dreadful a vision he is—whether he actually
appears like an "AIDS zombie," or whether it is the actor's physical bearing which
conveys BUCK's poor state of health: his weak posture, his languid and exhausted
movements, his eyes. BUCK is certainly not dressed for a leather bar. Instead, he
wears trousers which are now too large for him, a ragged down coat, and a long,
dirty scarf. His hair is long, thin and unkempt. DOG does not see him yet. BUCK
stands looking around for a bit, spots DOG, and then chooses to lean up against the
S R meatrack, by the door, his hands in his coat pockets. He looks again at DOG, and
directs all his lines to him, across the bar, starting up as the last howl fades. DOG, of*

course, does not hear him, and is, perhaps, jiggling obliviously to the now unheard beat.)

BUCK: It's a full moon above us. It pulls at the juices in the body. It pulls at the juices of the brain, makes a person restless, that moon. That's what. That's what. You won't find peace tonight, Dog. Not tonight, not under that moon. Look at me, Dog. I'm here.

(DOG, restless and distracted, shifts and looks around the bar. He accidentally locks gazes with BUCK for a moment, and stiffens.)

DOG: *(To himself, though still looking at BUCK)* He's here. He's in here.

(He nods at BUCK to acknowledge the gaze, then turns away, towards the audience, though he does not yet establish contact with us.)

BUCK: *(To DOG, as always)* It's a wilderness, Dog. You can erect a wall between us, but we're still in that same wilderness, beneath that moon.

DOG: *(To the audience)* Cruel. It must be odd for him to be in here. It must be hard. Why *is* he here? Not that he shouldn't be. It's his right, of course. But still, why? Maybe it's dementia. Half the time I think *I* might be demented. Or slipping. What would I do? Would I come here? I might—why not? *(Pause)* But why? *(Pause)* I don't even know why I am here *tonight*. Maybe I should go. This isn't working. *(Pause)* But I won't look at him again.

BUCK: Until I tell you to, Dog.

DOG: *(Defensively)* Why should I? After all, I *don't* know him. I don't mean to be unfriendly, but how much can a guy take? And what could I say, anyway? "Hi! Remember me? I'm the guy who slipped a twenty-dollar bill into your cigar box a couple of years ago"—? *(Ironically)* That's an opening!

BUCK: But you *do* know me, Dog. It's just that you don't know that you do, or won't let yourself. I'm Buck. Remember Buck? Fuck-a-Buck?

DOG: It *does* hurt. It *is* cruel. In a way, he shouldn't be in here. Nobody is going to talk to him. It's not just me. But nobody's to blame. He isn't to blame either.

BUCK: It's my *identity*, Dog. That's why you don't recognize me, why you don't see me when you look at me, why you didn't even see me on Castro Street the time you gave me that twenty-dollar bill. I have a new identity. I know that. *(Little laugh)* Why, used to be I scarcely recognized *myself* when I looked into the mirror. Just couldn't believe it, you know?

DOG: Is there any reason to assume he wants to talk to anyone anyway? Can't really talk to anyone in this place anyway, the music's so loud. So should I be friendly, pretend nothing's unusual about the situation, try to make him feel—what?

BUCK: Human?

DOG: Human. Maybe take my jacket off casually, so he can see I've got lesions on my arms. Tell him I go by the name of "Spot." Let him know he's not alone. *(Pause)* Of *course* he's not alone. This *is* San Francisco, after all. He must know, like I know, that at least half these guys—well, even if they're not showing any symptoms...

BUCK: Yeah, I know. Course I know. But it makes a difference when you can still *think* you're healthy, even if you know you're probably just fooling yourself. And it makes a difference when you can still *pass* for healthy, even when you know you aren't. There's a difference of *identity*, Dog.

DOG: Time was...before *I* got the Diagnosis, time was if a guy told me he'd been diagnosed, there was something I used to say. Words I had ready, I guess. Words I *meant*, though. I'd tell him, "Well, you know, we're *all* in this together." And I *did* mean it. And it *is* true. But funny thing: when I got the Diagnosis myself, I stopped saying that. I sure as hell didn't say it to anyone who *didn't* have the Diagnosis, even though I still believe it. But it seemed—it seems—discourteous.

BUCK: That's it. That's it. Courtesies are walls we erect in this wilderness, to protect *everyone* involved. Except those we shut out. That's it.

DOG: In a way, maybe it's—*discourteous* of this guy, this ghost, to walk in here. Maybe that's the worst you can say.

BUCK: But *you* brought me in here, Dog. You're why I'm here, dear. Look at me.

(DOG nervously looks around, and finds his eyes locked with BUCK's.)

BUCK: *(Gently)* That's right. That's it.

(Perhaps a gentle music underlies the following scene. The bar fades, and DOG and BUCK are alone together in a different, fantasy world. The time shown on the digital clock does not change. Both men stand tall, and begin by unconsciously taking the open, expectant stance of the kouros, looking at each other across the stage with Archaic smiles expressing their full presence for each other. During the course of the scene, BUCK builds his intensity gradually, as if he were fucking DOG with his words and his eyes, while DOG becomes more and more tense and breathless.)

BUCK: Yes, look at me, Dog.

DOG: It could be, it could have been...

BUCK: It was. It was only a few times, a few sweet fucks.

DOG: I can imagine he was beautiful. A beautiful man.

BUCK: The spring of '77, Dog.

DOG: It could be we would have met, years and years ago...

BUCK: A Saturday afternoon, Dog, in Buena Vista Park. Happened to be a full moon.

DOG: His slender, firm hips, his chest, his furry belly: I can imagine I would have—

BUCK: There were no walls between us then.

DOG: —I would have gone *wild*!

BUCK: And that was the point: the walls were down. You sucked me off, I sucked you off. We kissed and mixed our sweet cum, and we were both still hard, Dog, both still hard.

DOG: I can imagine...I can remember what it used to be like: I would have been mad to *smell* him, press my face into his belly, nuzzle down, breathe in...

BUCK: And we shoved our sticky hard-ons back into our jeans, and buttoned up with cummy fingers, and we nodded to each other and parted, each wandering off into that golden afternoon to see what *else* we could find, our happiness ran that high. Or maybe it was the moon.

DOG: Why do I know what his cock is like? Am I remembering it, or just imagining it?

BUCK: But then a week later—was it?—we recognized each other at the Safeway—

DOG: A strong cock...

BUCK: And you came back with me, to my studio in the Mission, and we fucked all afternoon and all that night, and on into the next afternoon. We nested in those cum-stiff greasy sheets and just couldn't leave each other alone: we needed more, more.

DOG: A strong cock, thicker at the head...I would suck at its root, my nose buried in his balls. And he'd squirm and cry, but I'd hold his hips down and dig in deeper with my tongue. It could be it was that way...

BUCK: And before we parted—

DOG: So maybe I would have fucked him, then, just using spit.

BUCK: Before we parted we planned to get together a third time, and we did, and it was cozy and sweet and fun... But familiarity was a factor, now, and the holy madness which impelled us to break down all walls between us had been satisfied, in our case. Its work was done. We both knew we wouldn't fuck together again, and that was fine, that was as it should be. Our spirits were enthralled with the dream of breaking down *all* walls between *all* men. So many men, so little time—remember? Fuck a guy, find his beauty and touch it, share.

DOG: And maybe we'd lie together for a bit, and then he'd turn me over and begin licking my ass... Maybe a finger, then, up my ass, and then another, sliding in and sliding out, loosening my asshole, loosening me...

BUCK: And we saw each other then, from time to time our paths happened to cross, usually at the full moon, and we'd smile at each other, knowing what a good thing we'd had together, and it was good to remember.

DOG: His cock, then, pushing in, and it hurts.

BUCK: And then that faded. I moved. I spent some years in Texas, then, and then in Jacksonville. And that's when I got ill, and that's when I came back. I could afford a bus ticket.

DOG: It hurts, but I let go, and he shoves his cock in: it's there, it's there—ah!

BUCK: A city is made of walls. That's it: that's a city, those walls, and artificial lights. But the wilderness is there all along anyway. Sit on a sidewalk. Sit out there on a sidewalk, and you'll see it, that wilderness. It's *inside*. It's inside *people*. You can see it in their eyes. That wilderness is inside everyone in this city. That's what I saw. I had forty dollars in my pocket when I got back, and that didn't last long.

DOG: His cock is there, inside me, and I breathe into the pain, let it be me...

BUCK: (*As if thrusting to climax*) And that's when I saw you again: I saw that twenty-dollar bill in my cigar box and I looked up to see who put it there, and I saw you: *you*, Dog. But I saw that you did not want to see *me*, that that twenty-dollar bill was a wall you were erecting, that the purpose of that twenty-dollar bill was to buy you *blindness*, to buy you blindness in the light of day.

DOG: (*Raising his head more and more, but still locking his gaze on* BUCK's *eyes; breathless*) And then it swells inside me: your urgency merges with my pain; a dark, unknown part of being floods rapidly through our bodies; each cell and sinew surrenders—

BUCK: Blind Dog! Blind Dog!

DOG: (*His head thrown back; losing eye contact with* BUCK) And then I can't— I can't—!

BUCK: But blind Dog *knows*: he can't buy himself out of this one after all:

DOG: It's—that's it: I—

BUCK: (*Very intensely, but not shouted*) I AM YOU, DOG:

DOG: (*Orgasm; staggering blindly a few steps towards* BUCK) I...! You...! Buck! Buck!

BUCK: (*Quietly, but still very intensely*) That's it, Dog: I...am...your...*ghost*!

DOG: (*Lowering his head to look again at* BUCK, *not comprehending*) Was your name Buck? *Is* it?

BUCK: (*Softer*) I...am...your...ghost.

DOG: (*Recoiling, staggering slightly backwards*) Is it? Is it?

BUCK: *(Whispered)* I...am...your...*ghost.*

(BUCK *holds for a few beats, and then suddenly turns and exits. The moment he does so, the clock begins again, flashing the new minute, and the horrifying music of the opening returns full force. DOG is standing S L, at the position he took before BUCK entered, his head bowed. Eventually he raises his head and looks out at the audience. The music stops. DOG glances over to where BUCK was standing, and then looks back at the audience.)*

DOG: He's gone.... *(Pause)* I'm relieved. I know I shouldn't be, I know it's wrong, but I am. There's only so much—grief you can allow into your life beyond a certain point. I don't know what happens to the grieving that *isn't* done: maybe it stays inside us, undone, waiting, maybe eating at us, like a wolf inside us. *(Pause)* Or maybe it turns us into wolves: I hope I never see this guy again. And that's—what is that?—that's nothing but the instinct for self-preservation. It's selfishness, but it might be necessary. There's too much fucking tragedy. And I've got commitments to guys I *do* know, people I know, and—you probably know what it's like—even *that* is using me up. I feel like I'm making excuses for myself. I know I'm betraying this guy. *(Pause)* No—I'm not betraying this guy, but something bigger. Something bigger, but what is it? I'm betraying—a dream, a dream, I used to have: I'm pretending I never had this dream, because it doesn't fit in nowadays, there's no place for it. Things are different, everything's changed. *(Pause)* Times change. Times change. That's it.

(He *looks down at his empty Calistoga bottle. As soon as he breaks contact with the audience the harsh music starts up again. The lights begin to fade. The digital clock begins to speed up: first a minute goes by for every measure of the music, then twice a measure, then on every beat, and then, as the stage becomes black, in blur. The music halts. We hear a final coyote howl, and the digital clock blinks out.)*

END OF PLAY

THE DEPLORATION
OF ROVER

CHARACTERS & SETTING

FIDO
DOG
ROVER

Castro Street, San Francisco; an evening in 1989

(Lights up on FIDO, *standing D S L.* FIDO *is a fat faggot in his forties. He has at least a moustache and perhaps a beard. He is dressed casually, with a light jacket— it is evening in San Francisco. He is discovered just about to light up a joint; he looks up at the audience after he has struck his match.)*

FIDO: *(To the audience)* You don't mind if I relax a bit, do you? *(He takes a toke and holds it in, smiling agreeably at the audience, then lets his breath out.)* End of a long day. *(He takes another toke and looks out at the audience as he holds it in again, this time with a worried, tense expression; he exhales.)* Quite a day. *(He takes a final toke. While he holds it in he occupies himself with carefully pinching out the roach and folding it into a scrap of paper, which he puts into his pocket. He exhales and looks up at us again.)* So! Time for a walk, okay? Time for your evening walk!

(The lights gradually come up on the set, representing storefronts on Castro Street at night. The set may be quite simplified and semi-abstract, but it should have the small-town feeling of the Castro, as well as its prettiness and wit. FIDO *has been watching the street come into view. Then, to the audience again:)*

FIDO: The Castro. *(Pause)* About ten years ago there was *such* a party here! Such madness, such joy! A big coming-out party for a million guys!— it *seemed* like a million. And one way of looking at it would be to see it as a party for *everybody,* for all of humanity—because the breakthrough we'd made *was* for all of humanity, or so some of us thought. But another way of looking at it—well, let's say there never was exactly a place for *me* in that party, not for guys like me, and, frankly, in those days I tended to *avoid* Castro Street. It was for beautiful guys, and the beauty hurt. It dazzled the eyes. But it hurt more than the eyes. It was—it always *will* be—like it made a hole, here *(Thumping his chest with his fist twice),* an ache, a yearning. I'll bet you know what I mean. *(Lets his hand drop from his chest)* Be that as it may, that was then, and this is now, and quite a few years ago I moved near Castro Street, a place on Diamond, and the move was right for me. It's become *my* neighborhood. And my neighborhood has been through a *lot,* over the years. A lot of changes. It sure ain't what it was, and I don't expect it ever will be again. But I think—I like to think—that there's a joy here again, a type of joy, even in these times, and a justifiable pride. Because we've proved ourselves. Times are hard. Times are going to be hard for a long while yet. But we're seeing it through. We're going to be here when the hard times are over: we're going to make it through. *(Pause)* And, you know one thing I love to see? Young people. Young gay people are still coming to San Francisco, for the same basic reason they did before: because our love is allowed here—or, at least, more allowed here than anywhere else. We've made that space for ourselves, for our lives, for our loves, and *nobody* is going to take it from us. This is still the best place in the world for us to be—*especially* in these times. And young gay people know it. So things are looking up on Castro Street, despite the losses—the many losses— and all the changes. Shall we take our walk?

(*He smiles at the audience, and then begins to saunter across the stage. As he approaches C S, the lights come up on a window display in one of the storefronts: a small easel holds the framed photograph of a man, with a small hand-lettered placard resting underneath it; next to the easel is a gorgeous bunch of yellow roses in a vase.* FIDO *spots the display and stops in his tracks, a bit stunned. To the photograph:*)

FIDO: Oh! *(Pause; sadly)* So you're dead too, now? *(Pause)* We never met. I never knew you. Never even knew your name. Until now. Hmmm! Rover. Rover: 1947 to 1989. That's all. God, you were *beautiful*, Rover! Talk about that ache! Talk about that yearning! *(Unconsciously bringing his hand to his chest)* Talk about that gaping *hole*! Whoever you were, Rover, I loved you, I envied you, I desired you, I hated you, I would have died just to have touched you once. To die for, to die for. And now *you're* dead.

(DOG, *also out for a stroll, enters S L, unseen by* FIDO. *He is a forty-five-year-old San Francisco faggot. He overhears* FIDO's *next lines, and stops behind him.*)

FIDO: And pretty roses. Yellow roses. Wonder what *that* means!

DOG: It means what you think it does.

FIDO: *(A bit startled; looking behind him at* DOG) Piss?

DOG: The Golden Shower Queen of All Time.

(FIDO *looks back at the display, which has him in thrall. Throughout their conversation both men mostly gaze at the display.*)

FIDO: Huh. You knew him.

DOG: Yeah. Did you?

FIDO: No. Just used to see him around. A lot.

DOG: Yeah.

FIDO: Beautiful guy.

DOG: Yeah, I guess. *(Shaking his head) Shit.* I heard he was sick, and I wanted to get in touch with him, and now it's too late. *Shit.*

FIDO: I'm sorry. It happens that way sometimes.

DOG: I know, I know. *(Pause)* But I hate it.

FIDO: Yeah.

DOG: We were roommates for a while, back in the Seventies. Party, party, party! Rover knew how to *party*!

(Pause)

FIDO: *(Turning to* DOG*)* You know, I work out at San Francisco General, Ward 86. And I see *awful* things every day. Young guys turning into old men right in front of your eyes.

DOG: Yeah?

FIDO: And young lives just about destroyed, kids coming in from the streets sometimes so messed up and so sick there just isn't much hope, not much hope left at all for them, they're jittery, crazy messes, and that's all.

DOG: Yup. I know.

FIDO: And not just gay guys, of course. At General we get *everyone*. All types. God, today there was a young woman, *so* young, and pregnant, and she was so fucking scared—you could see it in her eyes. Just wanted to *hold* her, like a child.

DOG: Yeah?

FIDO: Sorry to go on like this. It's just that it *still* gets me. *(Turning back to the window display)* I mean *this*. I'm just walking down the street, you know, and here it is. A guy I didn't even know but used to see around. And I loved him in a way. Anonymous love. Chances are I'll find out more about him than I ever knew before now that he's *dead*, if somebody puts an obit in for him, into the *B A R.*

DOG: Yeah. *(Pause)* I loved him too, I guess. Which maybe was harder since I knew him. No, that's not fair. I *did* love him. *And* it was hard. So hard I eventually gave up. But I know what you mean: he *was* beautiful. *(Pause)* But not pretty. It wasn't pretty. Being beautiful wasn't pretty for Rover.

FIDO: Oh?

DOG: Oh. But he held me once. We never fucked. But he held me all night, once, when I needed it, needed it badly, needed to be held. I cried and cried in his arms, and he let me. Shit. He wasn't a bad guy—far from it. He didn't have any meanness, not at all.

FIDO: What happened?

DOG: *(A bit defensively)* The time I was crying?

FIDO: Well, no—what happened between you two? Do you mind my asking?

DOG: *(Pause; sigh)* A lot of things. *(Pause)* I cleaned up my act, for one thing, and he kept on partying. And, hell, it was drugs, too: speed. Hate to say it, but that's part of what made him so beautiful: that fantastic energy. But you always reach a point, with anyone who's on that stuff, where you *can't* care any more, because caring means hoping, and after a point there *isn't* any hope, just like you say with those street junkies.

FIDO: You do what you've gotta do, but there's almost no hope. Maybe a few can be saved. You've gotta remember that.

DOG: And he had his ways, too. I could never figure out whether he was manipulating people deliberately or not. When I had to cut myself off from him because of the speed, I was *sure* it was deliberate. I had to hate it. But I don't know. He had those *orphan* eyes, you know. He couldn't help *that*.

FIDO: Yeah?

DOG: We used to joke about his orphan eyes, when there was something he wanted. But he *was* an orphan, or half an orphan. Raised by his grandparents up in Sonoma or Napa, somewhere around there.

FIDO: Half orphan?

DOG: He never knew who his father was. And his mother committed suicide when he was eight. He found her. She gassed herself, stuck her head in the oven.

FIDO: *(Under his breath)* Jesus.

DOG: It was her parents who raised him. Religious types, real hell-and-damnation fundamentalists. He always said he was lucky to escape that, but maybe he didn't after all. Maybe they succeeded in doing the same number on him that they did on his mother, eventually. I don't know.

FIDO: Could be.

DOG: So you had to have a little compassion when he used those orphan eyes on you. The hurt was real. I guess I never *really* doubted that. But I had to block it, couldn't think about it. Because if you look at it one way, it reached a point where what he was really asking was for you to push him a little deeper into hell. That's the way I came to see it, at least. Those orphan eyes...

FIDO: It's godawful sad. I didn't know.

DOG: And talented, too: a really talented guy. That was part of the tragedy, I guess. Not that any of it would have been any prettier if it'd happened to a guy with less ability. But he was valedictorian of his high school class, and he was putting himself through college when the draft decided to do away with student deferments and started that lottery business—remember?—and his number came up. He was a medic in Vietnam. And when that was over he didn't go back to college. He didn't do anything with his life. Except party. He was in New York for a couple of years when the party was just getting going there, and then he came back here. With his tambourine. He got by with one job or another—he could do *anything* he wanted, and do it well—and he partied, partied, partied. And that's his life story. That's what all his ability came to: the funnest party guy ever, and the Golden Shower Queen of All Time, lifting his leg all over this town. Now you know.

FIDO *(Making a rueful face at the photo)* Now I know. *(Sigh)* Oh, geez.

(Pause)

DOG: And I don't think he could stop. As I said, *I* stopped: I cleaned up my act. Though not in time, as it turns out. Still, there's some comfort in knowing that when I figured out what was happening, back in 1981— I mean AIDS, of course—I stopped, and I didn't, you know, spread it anymore. Safe sex. Or no sex. But not Rover. He kept right on playing. He could come up with any number of reasons.

FIDO: Yeah?

DOG: Yeah. At first he was fond of pointing out that those who were saying we shouldn't be having sex and who were, you know, trying to close the baths and all that—they were the same people who were railing against sex and the baths *anyway, before* anyone had heard of AIDS. His attitude was that if we'd all done what we were *supposed* to do, there wouldn't have been any gay life at all. And there's a certain logic to that. Gay life, gay liberation, *all* of this...well, the gay pioneers *were outlaws*, after all.

FIDO: There's more to it than that.

DOG: Oh yeah, I agree. Of course. A lot more. We can see that *now*. But, still, Rover had his point. And then there was a certain logic to the next line he took up: that we'd all heard the same message about safe sex plenty, and that anyone who chose to fuck with him knew just as well as he what the risks were, and that it was their own choice, and nobody else's business.

FIDO: *(Very bitterly)* And I deal with the result of that "logic" every day. And I'll *be* dealing with it for years to come, probably.

DOG: I never accepted that logic myself. But that was Rover. And I expect he suffered for it, too.

FIDO: *(Relenting)* Yeah.

(Pause)

DOG: I hope he didn't suffer much.

FIDO: Yeah. Well, that's a pretty futile thing to hope when there's so *much* suffering everywhere. And *nobody* deserves it.

DOG: I know, I know. *(Pause)* Well... *(To the photo)* Yeah, he *was* a beautiful guy. Some of the best times of my life were with him: the partying *was* wonderful, just incredible, beyond *anything*. And looking back at it now, I can't exactly put it down, I can't say I'm sorry. And he was a good guy, really. He had a good heart, one of the best. He was generous. He *shared* the good things, the fun. *(Pause)* And there was that time he held me. *(Pause; very softly)* Goodbye, Rover.

(The two men stand in silence for a while, gazing at the photograph. DOG sighs tensely, and wipes away a tear. FIDO, aware of movement behind him, turns and sees DOG's sorrow; immediately takes him into a warm hug and holds him while he cries silently. DOG then pulls himself together, and loosens the hug a bit by his breath; FIDO responds to the signal, but still holds DOG by the shoulders. Looking FIDO in the eyes and shaking his head slightly)

DOG: It's not just Rover.

FIDO: I know. *(Pause)* But there's some hope, now. There's light at the end of the tunnel. We're gonna make it through, some day.

DOG: Some of us are.

FIDO: *(Nodding)* Uh-huh.

(He gives DOG a final squeeze and releases him.)

DOG: Thank you.

FIDO: *(Drawing the encounter to a close, probably)* My name's Fido.

DOG: Hi. Friends call me Dog. Good meeting you.

FIDO: Say hi another time, okay?

DOG: Yeah. *(Pause)* Good night. *(Pause)* Thank you again, for the hug.

FIDO: Take care. *(Throws a little kiss)*

(DOG nods and exits, S R. FIDO watches him depart, then turns back to the photograph.)

FIDO: You beauty.

(There is the sound of a distant tambourine.)

FIDO: You beauty.

(ROVER appears. In a proper production, this will be in the display case, and his image will replace the easel and photograph, while the roses stay in place; this is "Pepper's Ghost Illusion," of course, and requires a large, expensive, fragile and awkward sheet of glass. Otherwise, perhaps a scrim can be used, or perhaps the lights come up on him in his own area of the stage, S R. He is facing us with his head bowed, and his hands together in front of him. He is wearing only beltless jeans, which ride his slender hips, and his body is lean and muscular, with steel tit rings; he is glistening with sweat and panting—we have caught him during a momentary pause in his dance. He raises his head slowly during FIDO's next few words, and we see that he has close-cropped hair and a full moustache, perhaps a beard or at least several days' growth of beard. FIDO, enthralled, speaks as if reciting a prayer to the vision.)

FIDO: So you went off to play...while I stayed home and guarded the bones...

(ROVER *unfurls the large gold fans he is holding, and dances. His dance is astoundingly intense and ecstatic; he is totally absorbed in it, totally narcissistic.* FIDO *continues his prayer.*)

FIDO: I loved your beauty. And I'll admit that if I'd had your beauty I might have gone off to play, too. But I loved your beauty because— *(Pause)* because it lit up the world, so brightly, lit up *my* life, *too*, and because— *(Pause)* because I *knew*. I *knew* you had that *same yearning I had*, that same gaping, aching hole, right *here (Striking his chest with his fist once)*, the pain. *(Pause; letting his hand drop)* That doesn't exactly justify anything you did, of course. I won't say that. But...I don't know the right or wrong of it all, I really don't. A guy can light himself up and go off like a Roman candle, and be very beautiful, and give off a *brilliant*, blinding light. And maybe it's hellfire for him, and maybe it isn't. Maybe there isn't any right or wrong about it. Maybe there's just joy and sorrow. I don't know. I don't know. I don't know. "I will not argue the matter..."

(ROVER's *dance comes to an end, and he folds his fans as the sound of the distant tambourine fades. He stands panting, and then slowly looks over and sees* FIDO *as if from a great distance or great height. Moving as if mesmerized, he squats to pick a yellow rose from the vase, stands again, and, miraculously, hands the rose to* FIDO *through the window of the display.*)

ROVER: *(Panting still; endearingly)* Speed...performs...miracles. *(He recedes and begins to fade.)*

FIDO: *(Holding the rose, as the vision fades; the cry of his heart)* Love performs miracles! *Love* performs miracles!

ROVER: *(Just before he fades away, still panting)* Then...the lover...is...blessed!

(ROVER *disappears into darkness.* FIDO *looks down at his rose as the lights fade.*)

END OF PLAY

HOLD

CHARACTERS & SETTING

LAD
DOG

DOG's *apartment by Buena Vista Park, San Francisco, 1989*

(Dog's apartment. S R is a bay window facing out to the audience; moonlight streams in the window and lies in a pattern across the floor. S L is Dog's bed and a small bedside table; a candle is lit on the table. Dog stands at the window, looking out. Lad is in bed, naked, sitting up, with the covers up to his waist.)

LAD: In this dream I am driving north, out of the city. What am I leaving behind? What is the city? Is it endurance? Is it stone? I don't know. I need to think. I need clarity, light. I need to breathe. The city has turned my lungs to stone.

(Pause)

DOG: *(Looking out the window as always, and never at LAD)* Is that you, Lad?

LAD: *(A lovely, low chuckle)* Always was, Dog.

DOG: Even now?

LAD: *(That chuckle again, for an answer)*

(Pause)

DOG: You were dreaming?

LAD: In this dream I need to see. I need to be free of the city, away.

DOG: *(With a touch of irony)* You were going away, all right. Further and further away.

LAD: North, out of the city. The bridge is so heavy with cars, and we move so slowly! All heading north, away, away. I can't move this weight, this metal and glass, this gasping engine! I am in the car beside me too, and in the car behind me, and all of us want to get off this bridge. But we move so slowly! And then, after hours have passed, at last we are free from the bridge! And the highway is ahead of us! We press our accelerators to the floor, we roar up the hill. Three lanes. Traffic loosens, but not enough: if anyone should make a mistake now—change lanes and cut off another car, swerve, lose control—there'd be no helping it: tons and tons of metal and glass smashed! But we hurtle on expertly, so smoothly... Miles and miles and miles. But in this dream the city still holds on: too many people, too many cars, too many shopping plazas and luxury boutiques, too many strip malls. Radio Shacks, Dunkin' Donuts, too many supermarkets, too many multiplex cinemas—that crap! That endless crap! This may be Marin, there may be money here, lots of it! But these are the slums, the slums of the mind, the slums of the spirit! Think what human life *is*, and then think that human creatures should choose to create this crap for their realm! Something is wrong. Too many people!

DOG: You're one of them.

LAD: *(Chuckle)* I was, yes. Too many people, though, too much despair.
If they believe anything at all other than what they see on their televisions,
they know something's wrong. If they have faith in anything with greater
meaning than this summer's blockbuster movies, they—all those people!—
they know something's *awfully* wrong.... Now we are speeding past their
houses, the tracts spread over the hills endlessly. All behind walls. There
is no dignity here. There can be no real chance. All of these homes for the
too-many people, all of these homes with their televisions bludgeoning
the too-many minds, deadening the too-many hearts! No, we all know
something is wrong. I drive on. I must be rid of it to see. At the end of this
dream I will see, I will be where I can see.

DOG: Huh. It didn't seem that way to me.

LAD: *(The simplest of explanations; "What did you expect?")* I left you in the city.
Maybe I had to be alone. Shall I go on?

DOG: Your dream?

LAD: Yeah.

DOG: Yeah.

LAD: *(With growing elation)* It must be for days and days, then, and I'm still
driving north. But it's all one day, too, one very long day, because night
does not come, not yet. I don't know how this can be, but now the light is
coming from the north: the further north I drive, the more I am facing into
the sun. I am the only one on this road, now, at last. It's winding through
pine forests, deep, deep, green and lush. The air is clear—it's what I need to
breathe—but we are climbing and it gets even clearer and rarer and colder.
And then I'm beyond the tree line, and it's all rocks and sparkling snow and
blue sky, the mountains. The road I'm on will come to an end soon, but then
it's only a short hike, a path I know. I leave the car behind then, and I take
this path. Why do I know this path? Maybe I dreamed about this path
before, a long-ago dream; I *have* been here before, once. How could I have
forgotten? But I knew where I was going!

DOG: Where are you, then?

LAD: *(Great happiness; sitting up with his feet over the edge of the bed)* Ah! I am
standing on a rock, a great rock, and *all* around me are the mountains, on all
sides! Craggy, raw mountains! *New* mountains, in geological time! *(Standing
up naked by the bed)* I stand, a man! I can see! I can breathe! The air is so pure!

DOG: And the sun?

LAD: *(Enthralled)* The sun is ahead of me, due north! And now it is setting!
I wish you could see the air here! It is *unbelievably* clear, like nothing you've
ever seen! So clear the first stars are out before the rim of the sun slips

behind the mountains! The air is thin, sharp! And the stars, then! Dog, Dog! You should *see*!

DOG: I'm looking at the stars now.

LAD: Ah, but those are over the city!

DOG: This is a city where you *can* see the stars, some of them.

LAD: They are *nothing* like these! I have never seen stars like these! Over the mountains! But there's more, Dog: something wonderful happens, but it's something that must be. It's why I needed to be free, it's why I needed this infinite space. *(With tears)* Oh God, at last! At *last*! My brothers! My brothers are there! Standing by me on that mountain! They are *there*! Their deaths— *(Pause)* in the city, their deaths were too *many, far* too many; the terror was too great, time gnawed at my heart. Even through years and years of their deaths, day by day, I could not comprehend, could not see! But *now*! These are the men I've loved, and now they stand by me on that rock! I know each one!

(He has taken a step or two towards DOG, *who still looks out the window; radiantly)*

LAD: And that is the dream. Remember the stars, Dog!

(Pause. DOG *kicks off his shoes. During his speech he will undress, leaving his clothes, folded, in a pile on the chair by the window or on the floor.* LAD, *a few paces behind him, is still, listening.)*

DOG: *(Still looking out the window)* So you were dreaming, Lad. I hope that is so. I cannot know. *(Pause; with difficulty)* But...Lad—I'll tell you a— a different story. About how...you went away. It's not to—contradict your story, your dream. It's just to put beside it, how it was for those of us you—didn't take with you. And we...we *weren't* dreaming, Lad. *(Pause)* I love this city. I love the lights at night. *(Pause. He looks down, then out the window again, as he unbuttons his shirt.)* So, Lad...You went away. Little trips at first, little—lapses...What day was it? Tuesday?

LAD: "Oh? Were we going to have dinner?"

DOG: "Yes. Tonight. And the opera."

LAD: "I thought that was yesterday."

DOG: Little lapses, little confusions... "Confused" was the term we used. *(He takes his shirt off and folds it, putting it on the chair.)* No one wanted to say what we all knew. And at dinner that night...*(He pulls his undershirt off, over his head, and holds it.)* At dinner that night, yes, you looked awfully ill. But what was scary was—the way your talk laced through the conversation—so loosely, like a mayfly: touching lightly, touching lightly, and then—disappearing, just gone. *(He drops the undershirt on the chair.)* Leaving silences behind you. Your voice—I loved your voice, Lad, I loved those gentle inflections! And it *was* your voice, it *was* the same, *so* familiar it *had* to be you. *(Pause)* But where were you? You were not there. *(Unbuttoning and unbuckling his jeans)* You were not there with us at dinner that night. *(He strips his jeans and socks off, and piles them on the other clothing. He is standing in boxer shorts. His body, legs and arms are exotically spotted with a considerable number of Kaposi's Sarcoma lesions.)* I hated correcting you when you were—mistaken, confused. Contradicting you was not—was not something I had ever done before, we had no—*way* between us for that, and it puzzled you. Perhaps you sensed something was wrong then. I don't know. Three times during the opera you began to talk over the music—

LAD: *(Rather loudly)* "Did you write this music?"

DOG: *(Whispered)* "Shh! No! No!"

LAD: "I thought you did."

DOG: *(As before)* "Shh! No! Don't talk now!"

LAD: *(Softer, puzzled)* "Oh! I'm sorry!"

DOG: *(Normal voice)* And after the opera, then— "Where are you going?"

LAD: "To the car."

DOG: "But it's not down there. We parked on Franklin."

LAD: *(Irritated)* "It's in the basement! The garage!"

DOG: "Lad...I don't think there's a garage here at the Opera House. I think you've got that wrong. Anyway, the car's outside."

LAD: *(Upset)* "No! No!"

(Pause)

DOG: *(Softly, eyes closed, shaking his head.)* No. No. *(Pause; then an access of pain; crescendo)* No, no, no, no, *no!* *(Long pause; he looks out the window, calming his breathing and collecting himself from nearly breaking down. Then:)* And then the next Wednesday...you were missing. With your car. Without your medicines. Gone. No word to anyone. *(Pause)* Your roommate called me, wanting to know if I might have any idea where you were. He'd already called the police. There was nothing more to do. For two days we didn't know where you were. I didn't think you would commit suicide, but I didn't know. And here's where our two stories have a point of contact after all, because during those two days of waiting and worrying whether you were still alive, something in me *knew* you had driven north, out of the city; I kept thinking, for some reason, that that must be what you had done. And I was right. Friday they found you. *(Pause)* But you hadn't gotten that far. They found you somewhere in Marin, at the end of a dirt road. You had driven off into a ditch, and spent two days and two nights in that car. I don't know why you were still alive. They brought you back. *(Long pause.*

He strips off his shorts and drops them on the pile of clothing, and then stands gazing out the window again.) I love this city. I love the lights at night. *(Looking to his right)* The park here, masses of dark trees, and sometimes you see a cigaret end glowing in the darkness. *(To his left)* And then the city, to the south. *(Pointing right to left)* Market Street, bright. South of Market. The Mission. Potrero Hill...and those little toy buildings you can see at the base of the hill: San Francisco General. That's where you died. *(Eyes fixed on the spot as he lets his arm fall)* That's where guys are dying right now. Guys we've both loved. Too many of them. *(Pause)* Chances are, that's where *I'll* die, too.

(Pause. LAD *comes up behind* DOG *and embraces him from behind.)* I wish you were really here, Lad.

LAD: *(Softly)* I am. Always will be. Like the stars, Dog. Remember the stars.

DOG: I *do* remember the stars.

LAD: *(Looking up to his right, out the window)* There's the Dog Star.

DOG: *(Looking at the star)* Yes. I know.

LAD: Draw an imaginary line from you *(His pointing finger tapping* DOG's *chest; then pointing up at the Dog Star)* up to the Dog Star. Then draw another line down from the Dog Star to General *(Points downward over to his left, to San Francisco General Hospital)*. And draw a line from General back over here *(His pointing finger again on* DOG's *chest)*. Do you see a big triangle? You, the star, the hospital? Do you?

DOG: *(Softly)* Yeah.

LAD: The thing to remember is that it's only from here that it looks like a triangle. Because it isn't at all. It's an illusion. That Dog Star is so far away, so many, many light years, that any distance at all on this earth is nothing. And time is nothing.

DOG: *(Looking over at San Francisco General; pause)* That distance is *everything*, to me. It's all I have. And time is not nothing when it's all the time I have. It's life. It's all that matters.

LAD: *(Chuckles)* Hold onto the stars, Dog.

DOG: *(Pause; eyes cast down)* I wish you were really here, Lad. Your *body*, living. And your mind. *You: what you were.* And, yeah, that had something to do with the stars. But you: back, sharing this illusion with me, this space, this time. I wish I weren't just imagining the warmth of your belly against my back, your arms around me, your cock bobbing against my butt.

(LAD chuckles.)

DOG: Or touch. Just touch. Yeah, sure, hold onto the stars. But I miss *touch*. I wish I could hold onto you—hold onto *you*.

LAD: Mmmm. *(He chuckles; then kisses* DOG's *ear, loosens his hold on him and begins to back away)*

*(*DOG *stands with his arms folded across his chest, hugging himself, eyes still cast down. Pause)*

DOG: I know you're not here. You're not even a ghost. I'm just—*thinking* you. That's all the existence you have, now, all that's left of you: what you meant to others. *(Face up to the stars)* And that was good.

(Long pause while DOG *looks up;* LAD *disappears.* DOG *then looks over at San Francisco General Hospital.)*

DOG: A short distance. Maybe only a little time. *(He stands at the window a little longer, then crosses over S L to the bed, gets into bed, blows out the candle, and goes to sleep.)*

END OF PLAY